# CONTENTS

# Introduction to the Pesach Guide 5771

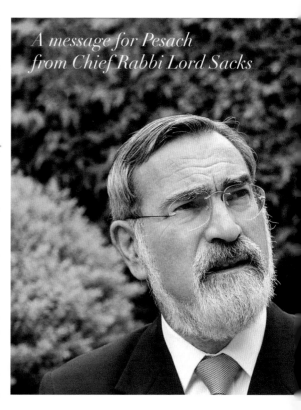

*A message for Pesach from Chief Rabbi Lord Sacks*

*"This Pesach, as we celebrate together, remember that the Seder service that begins with the words, 'This is the bread of affliction', ends with the wine of freedom and with a children's song in which God defeats the angel of death. No force has lasted as long as, or had greater influence on humanity than, the voice of Jewish hope. It was born when God told Moses, My name is Ehyeh asher Ehyeh, meaning: I am the God you will find if you have faith that the future can be different from the past."*

*'E*ven if we are all wise, all understanding, all people of experience, all learned in Torah, still we are under an obligation to speak about the exodus from Egypt, and the more we do so, the more we are worthy of praise.'

So says the Haggadah, and to an extraordinary degree it remains so. Still we tell the story, even though Jews have done so for thirty three centuries, making the Seder service almost certainly the oldest continuously observed religious ritual in the world. And still it fascinates, intrigues and engages us, because its themes are fundamental and constitute a challenge in every age, including ours.

It speaks about oppression, about an unfree society where the strong enslave the weak, and that has not ceased in parts of the world today where, for example, child labour is still common, or women deprived of rights. It speaks about the bread of affliction, and that too still exists in a world where a billion people live in abject poverty. It speaks about the long walk to freedom, and there are all too many places where the journey is still incomplete. The themes of the Exodus and of Pesach are universal and never exhausted. But they are also particular. They tell us what it is to be a Jew, not just a member of humanity in general. The Seder service is the way we hand our story on to the next generation, connecting it with the distant past ("This is the bread of affliction our ancestors ate in the land of Egypt") and a hoped-for future, when Elijah will come and tell us that the Messiah is on his way.

There never was a more beautiful way of giving our children their entry into identity than by insisting that the entire ritual be set in motion by the questions asked by a child. Nor is there a more powerful one than by re-enacting the formative events of our people, tasting the tastes, recalling the miracles, turning history into memory, as if we were there, caught as our ancestors were between fear and hope, and taking the risk of setting out on the journey of faith.

Somehow this most ancient story never ceases to be new. In fact as I write these words, there has been political ferment in the land of Egypt, with a new group of people demanding freedom from oppressive rule. Ancient history can sometimes speak more compellingly to the present than newspapers do.

Which is why I celebrate this excellent new Pesach guide and commend those who produced it. I hope it stimulates you to relate what happened then to what is happening now. I hope it inspires you to new thoughts, insights, and yes – even questions. For this is the never-ending story of the never-ending people made great by their never-ending faith.

Wishing you a Chag kasher vesameach,

Jonathan Sacks

Chief Rabbi Lord Sacks

# NISAN TIMELINE

For a brief description of many of these terms please see the Pesach overview and Living sections

## 14th
Searching for Chametz – Bedikat Chametz

Fast of the Firstborn - Ta'anit Bechorot

Stop eating Chametz
Burn the Chametz

## 15th
1st Seder night

## 16th
2nd Seder night
Begin counting the Omer

## 17th
Chol Hamoed 1
2nd day of the Omer

## 18th
Chol Hamoed 2
3rd day of the Omer

## 19th
Chol Hamoed 3
4th day of the Omer

## 20th
Chol Hamoed 4
5th day of the Omer

## 21st
7th day Pesach – Yom Tov
Song of the Sea
6th day of the Omer

## 22nd
8th day Pesach –
Yom Tov

Yizkor
7th day of the Omer

## Dates of first night Pesach

| | |
|---|---|
| 2011 | Monday 18th April |
| 2012 | Friday 6th April |
| 2013 | Monday 25th March |
| 2014 | Monday 14th April |
| 2015 | Friday 3rd April |
| 2016 | Friday 22nd April |
| 2017 | Monday 10th April |
| 2018 | Friday 30th March |
| 2019 | Friday 19th April |
| 2020 | Wednesday 8th April |

# Introduction

*By Rabbi Andrew Shaw, Director of US Living & Learning and Community Development Rabbi at Stanmore & Canons Park United Synagogue*

We hope you enjoy this second offering from the brand new Living & Learning Department of the United Synagogue. Our first publication, Guide to Tishrei was well received in over 25,000 homes at Rosh Hashanah and we hope the Guide to Pesach will have a similar response.

Since September, the department has grown and we were joined by Rabbi Michael Laitner as our Education Coordinator who has been responsible putting this Pesach guide together. As always the idea of the guide is to help link our members to relevant, meaningful and authentic Judaism for the 21st century.

Perhaps more than any other festival, Pesach is a time of family and friends getting together. We share the wonderful customs and traditions of Seder night, and if Sesame Street were bringing you Seder night, they would probably bring it to you with the number four! With that in mind, we have spilt this guide into four sections.

The first three are entitled Living, Learning and Caring – principles which guide the United Synagogue. The "Living" section contains articles that deal with understanding and preparing for Pesach. The "Learning" section contains various articles written about the festival of Pesach. What is special about this guide is that articles were written by both Rabbis and US members. The "Caring" section deals with various areas of Chesed (kindness) such as assistance for those in hospital over Pesach and ways you personally can make a difference this Pesach.

The fourth section is all about the Haggadah and is designed to be used during your Seder. We hope it will add to your all round experience. Further audio and written materials for Pesach are also available on the You&US website – www.theus.org.uk/you&us

I do hope you will find this guide a useful resource which helps you experience Pesach with more knowledge and inspiration, to last you through Seder nights and beyond

Chag Sameach

Rabbi Andrew Shaw

## Acknowledgements

**All of our writers;**
**The Chief Rabbi and the Office of the Chief Rabbi for their support;**
**The United Synagogue Trustees and Trustee Observers:** Dr Simon Hochhauser (President), Stephen Fenton, Geoffrey Hartnell, Stephen Pack, Russell Tenzer, Peter Zinkin, Dalia Cramer, Irene Leeman, Elaine Renshaw;
**The US Marketing Department for its design of this Guide:** Ian Myers, Richard Marcus, Ruth Millet and Josh Saunders;
**The US Community Services Department** led by David Kaplan for its assistance with ideas and the sourcing of articles;
**The Living & Learning team:** Rabbi Michael Laitner, Avi Friedmann and Joanna Rose.
Jeremy Jacobs, Sharon Laitner, Fiona Palmer and Saul Taylor for all their contributions to this project
**Credo for their kind sponsorship of this Guide**

# PESACH
# OVERVIEW

*Rabbi Michael Laitner, Education Coordinator of US Living & Learning, Assistant Rabbi of Finchley United Synagogue*

# What is Pesach?

Pesach (Passover in English) is our yearly commemoration of the Exodus of the Jewish people from Egypt, following our slavery there. The prelude to the Exodus was the famous ten plagues. Pesach is a moving, inspiring festival, whose messages of liberty and responsibility, ensconced in the way we celebrate the festival, have resonated with both Jews and non-Jews throughout the ages. Pesach marks the start of the consolidation of our nation status as the Jewish people.

This concept of individual and national freedom is but one of the revolutionary ideas that Judaism has given the world.

Traditionally, Pesach is a time when families and friends get together, particularly for the Seder nights which are the highlights of Pesach. Even if you celebrate Pesach by yourself, you are part of the whole Jewish people who as a collective group are celebrating Pesach with you.

In the words of Chief Rabbi Lord Sacks, "Pesach is the festival of hope, and Jews are the people of hope. For we are the people who outlived every empire that sought to destroy us, survived adversities that would have defeated any other nation, that emerged from the Holocaust still affirming life, and built the land and State of Israel against unceasing opposition."[1]

Lest we forget these lessons, the Haggadah, the text we use for the Seder, states that we must view ourselves as if we too left Egypt, not just our ancestors.

# When does Pesach start and how long does it last?

Pesach starts on 15 Nisan in the Jewish calendar, the anniversary of the very day that we left Egypt.

Pesach lasts for eight days outside of Israel and seven days in Israel. In the Diaspora (outside of Israel), the first two and last two days are "Yom Tov", holy days, whilst the days in between are semi-festive days called "Chol Hamoed". In Israel, the Yom Tov days are the first and last days of Pesach.

---

[1] Pesach message 2010/5770.

CHAMETZ
TO MATZAH

The festive Yom Tov days are similar in atmosphere and in Halacha (Jewish law) to Shabbat, whilst Chol Hamoed is a time when we can perform necessary weekday tasks whilst retaining the atmosphere of Pesach.

Although the Seder is the focus of the first Yom Tov part of Pesach, we also start to count the Omer on the second night of Pesach, counting each subsequent night up to 49 days in total. This counting links Pesach with the festival of Shavuot, which celebrates the revelation at Mount Sinai, seven weeks after the Jewish people left Egypt, and helps us to prepare for Shavuot. It is preferable to count at night, but you can also count during the day, albeit without the special blessing. See page 238 in the "green" version of the Singer's Prayer Book ('the green Siddur') for details.

On the last days of Yom Tov, the focus is on the famous splitting of the Reed Sea followed by Moses' song of thanks (described in Shemot/Exodus chapters 14 and 15). The Jewish people crossed the sea safely before the waters engulfed Pharaoh's army which was chasing the Jews with mortal intent.

As on any other Yom Tov, Kiddush is recited before the Yom Tov meals (pages 660 and 730 in the green Siddur) and we say special Yom Tov prayers. Yizkor memorial prayers are recited on the last day of Pesach. After nightfall at the conclusion of Pesach, we recite the Havdalah prayers which formally mark the conclusion of the Festival (page 608 in the green Siddur).

# What is Chametz and what is Matzah?

In its purest form, Chametz is a mixture of water with either barley, oats, wheat, rye, spelt or any derivative of these grains which has risen or fermented and has not been baked within 18 minutes from the time that the mixture was made. For the duration of Pesach we remove Chametz from our possession.

In practical terms, given the complexity of food production, all food that we own or eat on Pesach must be approved as "Kosher for Pesach" by a kosher certifier such as the Kashrut Division of the London Beth Din. See www.kosher.org.uk

In contrast to Chametz, we have a mitzvah (obligation) to eat Matzah. Matzah is a mixture of flour and water which has been baked within 18 minutes from the time the mixture was made. Matzah must also be certified as "Kosher for Pesach" by a kosher certifier. Before you buy, check the packet to make sure. Rakusens Matzot (plural of Matzah) are certified by the Kashrut Division of the London Beth Din. Look at the Rakusens website for more information about Matzah.

# LIVING SECTION

בְּכָל דּוֹר וָדוֹר חַיָב אָדָם לִרְאוֹת אֶת עַצְמוֹ
כְּאִלוּ הוּא יָצָא מִמִּצְרַיִם

*B'chol dor vador chayav adam lirot et atzmo k'ilu hu yatza mi-mitzrayim."*

*In every generation one is obligated to see oneself as if one who went out from Egypt.*

"It is not enough simply to learn about Pesach – we need to live it as well. It is a festival brimming with experiences that last a lifetime."

The quote above reminds us that Pesach is not simply a vital part of Jewish history but a central part of Jewish memory. As Chief Rabbi Lord Sacks has written, "History is someone else's story, memory is my story. In history we recall what happened. Through memory we identify with what happened so it becomes part of us and who we are. History is the story of a past that is dead. Memory is the story of a future."

Seder night is the annual retelling and in some ways the reliving of the original Pesach and Exodus.

So, enjoy the Living section of this Guide. Here you can find different ways to experience the festival, from ideas that engage children to Pesach customs from around the world.

# Getting ready for Pesach – (the countdown)

Pesach is a festival which requires preparation. Before Pesach, we either eat or remove Chametz that is in our possession by cleaning our homes. The Torah commands that we may neither eat, nor own, nor benefit from any Chametz on Pesach. Cleaning is required in any places where Chametz may have been during the rest of the year.

On Pesach, we do not use utensils that have been used with Chametz. Instead, we use utensils reserved for Pesach or utensils that have been "kashered" for Pesach under rabbinic supervision. Ask your local United Synagogue rabbi for guidance about "kashering" should you wish to do this.

Valuable items of Chametz, such as bottles of whisky, that you are unable to finish before Pesach and would suffer significant loss by abandoning, should be sold before Pesach to a non-Jew, through the offices of your local United Synagogue rabbi who uses a pro-forma sale procedure. These items are securely put away before Pesach and not consumed until after Pesach when the rabbi has reacquired them on your behalf.

To sell your Chametz online through the Kashrut Division of London Beth Din visit the United Synagogue website at:

**www.theus.org.uk/sellmychametz**

# Erev Pesach, the day before Pesach

On the night before Pesach, having prepared our homes for the festival, we conduct one final search for Chametz after nightfall. This search, which can be done in a cursory way, is a last check and an opportunity to make sure that any Chametz we sell before Pesach is securely put away.

Traditionally, it is conducted by candlelight with a feather and spoon which adds to the excitement of the experience, especially for children. Set aside any Chametz you find, or some you put aside before the search for the following morning when that Chametz is disposed of, finalising the removal of Chametz from our possession and preparing for us to enter Pesach in a spiritual sense by internalising the meaning of removing and stopping to eat Chametz. Look for instructions and the necessary declarations either in your Haggadah or on page 642 of the green Siddur.

There are deadlines for the final time to eat Chametz on the morning before Pesach and the final time to dispose of Chametz. Check your synagogue calendars for these times each year or look at the United Synagogue website.

PREPARE FOR SEDER

# The Fast of the Firstborn

Erev Pesach is also the Fast of the Firstborn ("Ta'anit Bechorot"), for male first borns over Barmitzvah age. One reason for this fast is for firstborns to show gratitude that their firstborn ancestors were spared during the plague of the firstborn preceding the Exodus from Egypt.

This fast though, is the most minor of fasts and attendance at a "Siyum" to celebrate the important occasion of completing a significant section of Jewish study overrides the fast. Speak to your local United Synagogue rabbi for more details about attending a Siyum or email the Living & Learning department at L&L@theus.org.uk if you are unable to contact your rabbi.

If the first Seder falls on Saturday night, there are changes to the procedure and timings from a weekday Erev Pesach. The Fast of the Firstborn is held on the preceding Thursday and the search for Chametz takes place on Thursday night after dark. Friday is treated as if it was Erev Pesach, although Chametz can still be eaten as that Friday is not actually Erev Pesach. For the Shabbat meals, the most practicable solution is to use egg matza instead of challa. Preparations for the Seder cannot begin before the end of Shabbat, so do as much as you can on Friday. See the article on the You & Us website providing further information for this situation.

# Preparing for the Seder

The Seder table needs to be laid. The Seder plate and the special Seder foods, need to be prepared. Ashkenazi practice is to avoid eating lamb at the Seder or any dry roasted meat. The Seder starts after nightfall. See the United Synagogue website or your local synagogue calendar for precise times.

Candles are lit to bring in each Yom Tov and Shabbat of Pesach just as they are before a regular Shabbat, but a special beracha (blessing) is said for Yom Tov candles. See page 644 in the green Siddur for the beracha and the United Synagogue website for the latest candle lighting times, which correspond to when Pesach begins. For more detail about this and how to light on the second days of Yom Tov, please see the You&Us website.

May you have an inspiring, enjoyable and meaningful Pesach celebrating the story of the Jewish people and your part in it, as Jews have done since that night in Egypt all those years ago.

# 5 CUSTOMS FROM AROUND THE WORLD

# Introducing 5 customs from around the globe to make your Seder night different from all other Seder nights

Collated by Joanna Rose of US Living & Learning

*1.* The Israelites crossed the Reed Sea on the seventh day of Pesach. Various Jewish groups commemorated this miracle by re-enacting the drama! Some people poured buckets of water on the floor of their house, creating a miniature "sea" and walked from one side of the room to the other. A more practical suggestion would be to step over bowls of water! **Sephardi Custom**

*2.* Redeeming Ourselves. Rabbi Naftali Tzvi Horowitz (1760-1827) invited Seder participants to pour wine from their own goblets into Elijah's cup. This symbolised the personal deeds and contributions that each person must make to bring redemption. When doing this, think carefully about what you, as an individual and as part of the Jewish people, can do to hasten future redemption.

*3.* A 'super sofa Seder' where most of the Seder is conducted with the participants reclining on bean bags and couches to enable them to lean more comfortably. A map is drawn up before Pesach starts, showing the journey Bnei Yisrael (the Children of Israel) took on their 40 years of wandering. Refer to the map as you go through the Haggadah. Use role playing (and even some dressing up!) if that will help to tell the Seder story in a more vivid way. **Finchley Custom**

*4.* When two families share a Seder for the first time, they sing different tunes and battle it out for who can sing the loudest! **Wembley Custom (based on the Stadium!)**

*5.* Heavy Charoset: the mixture of apples, nuts, cinnamon and wine, commemorates the bricks that Israelites made in Egypt, tastes earthier in some cultures. During America's Civil War, Jewish Union soldiers from Salonika, Greece, added chopped stone to their Charoset, and some Moroccans included grated rock. Though interesting, most people chose to abandon this custom and you can probably guess why! **North American & Moroccan Custom**

If you have a custom you'd like to share, please email us at L&L@theus.org.uk

\* This article was sourced from various websites, friends and work colleagues.

PREPARE
FOR PESACH

# A suggested Pesach Checklist

*Elisheva Schlagman, United Synagogue Community Division Assistant and Chair of Edgware United Synagogue's "Menucha VeSimcha" service*

## Before Pesach

1. Plan a cleaning schedule and allocate tasks;
2. Plan a shopping schedule;
3. Complete a sale of Chametz form;
4. Plan Pesach guest lists and menus. Think of people who may particularly appreciate an invite;
5. Look for an opportunity to help somebody else who needs assistance in preparing for Pesach, such as helping an elderly person with shopping;
6. Remember to prepare a Matzah-free lunch for Erev Pesach. We do not eat Matzah on Erev Pesach to make the Matzah taste fresher at the Seder;

## The Seder

1. Many Haggadot (plural of Haggadah) contain a picture illustrating the arrangement of the Seder plate to help you prepare the plate;
2. Make sure you have enough kosher for Pesach wine or grape juice;
3. Prepare a hand washing bowl;
4. Make sure you have three Shemura Matzot for the Seder plate and enough Shemura Matzot for each participant to consume for the Matzah, Korech and Afikoman parts of the Seder;
5. A vegetable such as parsley or celery to be eaten for the Karpas vegetable at the Seder (a different vegetable from that to be used for bitter herbs, see point 12 below);
6. Horseradish or bitter romaine lettuce leaves to serve as Maror (bitter herbs);
7. Salt for salt water;
8. A shank bone, roasted chicken bone or chicken neck for the Seder plate;
9. Prepare the charoset mixture using grated apples, red wine, cinnamon and ground almonds or other nuts;
10. A boiled, scorched egg for the Seder plate. You can roast the egg by singeing it a little bit with an open flame;
11. A wine cup for each participant. The cup should hold at least 86ml of which at least half should be drunk for each of the four cups. An average plastic cup holds approximately 200ml;
12. Cushions for leaning at the Seder, for those who wish to use them;
13. Make sure you have enough Haggadot for all those present at the Seder.

**And finally...find out when Pesach begins next year (!) by looking at the United Synagogue website's Jewish calendar.**

ENGAGE
PESACH

# Ten ways to engage children at Pesach time

*Rabbi Baruch and Rebbetzin Kezi Levin, Brondesbury Park United Synagogue*

*1.* Get your kids involved in the cleaning. Half the fun is in the preparation for Pesach. Let them bath with the lego, give them their own gloves, brooms, sponges and set them to work. The more you put in the more you get out!

*2.* Start the Seder by having each child prepare their own Seder plate. Do this at the table and discuss the significance of each item as you go along.

*3.* Have someone act as news reporter and every so often cross 'live to Egypt' to see what is happening to the Jews.

*4.* Get your kids to collect a bag full of odds and ends from around the house, for example a toy car, a drinking straw, a toothbrush, an envelope, a hat, pyjama trousers etc. Put them all in a bag and pass the bag round at the Seder table. Each person picks out an item without looking and then connects their object to the story of Pesach.

*5.* Let kids come up with a TV style commercial introducing each of the 10 plagues.

*6.* Buy small props to bring the ten plagues to life (e.g. plastic frogs, insects, toy animals, sunglasses for darkness, ping pong balls for hail) and scatter them on the table at the appropriate time.

*7.* Have a large set of lego or wooden blocks on the floor next to the Seder table and get the kids to build a pyramid whilst the adults read the 'long bits'.

*8.* In advance of the Seder prepare celebrity heads (write out on separate pieces of paper the names of characters or objects associated with Seder night, for example Matzah, Maror, Charoset, Pharaoh, Elijah the Prophet, The Wise Son, Frog, Wild Beast, etc). One person has the name of the character or object placed on their head without them seeing it and has to ask ten yes or no questions to try and discover their identity.

*9.* Do Chad Gadya using animal noises as you go along. After four cups of wine, these should sound quite real!

*10.* Let the kids stay up to the wee hours of the morning. Don't be precious about the time. These are the things that will remain in their memories forever!

# LEARNING SECTION

וְהָיוּ מְסַפְּרִים בִּיצִיאַת מִצְרַיִם כָּל אוֹתוֹ הַלַּיְלָה

# "Ve hayu mesaperim b'yitziat mitzraim kol oto ha'layla" – They were speaking about the Exodus from Egypt throughout the night.

Rabbi Andrew Shaw

As a child I had the '*Children's Hagaddah*' (who didn't?) where each year I would read the poem about the Rabbis in Bnei Brak – 'of Rabbi Eliezer a story is told' (complete if you can remember!) The picture in my mind then, and still to some extent now, is of the rabbis so engaged in Jewish learning and discussion that they completely failed to realise the time going by.

Jewish learning has always been and always will be a core value of our people. We have always prioritised the education of our community. As the Chief Rabbi wrote in his book, *Will We Have Jewish Grandchildren?*, "Judaism predicated its survival on education. Not education in the narrow, formal sense of the acquisition of knowledge but something altogether broader. Indeed the word 'education' is wholly inadequate to describe Judaism's culture of study, meditation and debate, its absorption in texts, commentaries and counter commentaries, its devotion to literacy and lifelong learning. Descartes said 'I think therefore I am'. A Jew would have said 'I learn, therefore I am'."

So we are not expecting you to stay up all night learning like the Rabbis of old, but we invite you to engage with the next section of this Guide, a challenging section. The four essays cover Jewish law, philosophy, history and prayer, written by a cross section of our community who are united in their love of learning and love of Pesach study in particular. As we say in the Haggadah, "Tzei Ulmad", go and learn!

INSIGHTS
INTO PESACH

# Pesach Q&A
## Rabbi Michael Laitner interviews Dayan Menachem Gelley, Senior Dayan of the London Beth Din.

### Why do I need to clean for Pesach and buy special "kosher for Pesach" foods? Is the cleaning the same as spring cleaning?

The Torah's prohibition of eating Chametz is particularly strict and includes foods which contain Chametz derivatives as well as pure Chametz. The prohibition of Chametz on Pesach is repeated in the Torah a number of times demonstrating its severity. Accordingly, we are particularly careful to ensure that we do not eat any Chametz at all on Pesach. This is the will of God as expressed in the Torah and we play by the "Book of Books". There are many insightful meanings to enhance our appreciation of Pesach; sometimes we can understand (to the best of our capacity) some commandments of the Torah more readily than others.

Pesach cleaning is not the same as spring cleaning. The two tasks should not be confused! In normal circumstances, there is no need for Pesach cleaning to be an onerous burden. On Pesach, we may not eat, own or benefit from Chametz. Therefore, we only need to clean to eradicate Chametz and do not need to clean where there is no Chametz. If one keeps a room Chametz free throughout the year, the room will not require cleaning for Pesach. Furthermore, the prohibition of owning Chametz does not apply to scattered crumbs, or those trampled into the ground as they are automatically nullified. Accordingly, other than for the kitchen no heavy duty cleaning should be required. It should be sufficient to vacuum and clean sofas etc.

Selling Chametz and nullification of any remaining Chametz also take care of any remaining Chametz that was not picked up during cleaning. There is therefore no need to be obsessive about Pesach cleaning.

### Do I really need "Kosher for Pesach" products for foods that do not contain Chametz, such as tea or sugar?

It is amazing how many seemingly innocuous products can contain Chametz. One frozen vegetable supplier that I visited, for example, aims to get products from the field to the supermarket shelf within six hours. Some products, such as certain frozen vegetables, are blanched in warm water to destroy damaging enzymes and bacteria. The blanching water contained pasta. The vegetables, by being cooked in warm pasta water, became top grade Chametz! This underscores the need for the professional advice that a Kashrut agency such as the Kashrut Division of the London Beth Din, can provide. Food technology is highly complicated.

We do strive to keep costs to a minimum and are delighted for the first time this year to certify regular Tate and Lyle castor and granulated sugar that can be purchased from a normal supermarket shelf as kosher for Pesach. Research at the relevant factories has satisfied our kosher for Pesach requirements in that neither the foods themselves nor the factory conditions have exposure to any Chametz. We hope to expand this to other staple products such as tea and salt etc.

## What should I do if I cannot afford Pesach foods?

Eat regular foods that are intrinsically kosher for Pesach such as vegetables, fish, eggs, fruit etc which can be used for many delicious Pesach recipes. There is no need to purchase expensive Pesach manufactured and processed foods. Eat simple foods with Matzah to avoid racking up costs to an unreasonable level.

## What is egg matzah and can I eat it on Pesach?

Chametz is made in its most basic form by mixing flour and water and leaving the mixture to rise for even a minimal period of time. Hence the skill in Matzah baking of placing the dough in the oven immediately after it has been kneaded without allowing it time to rise. Depending on the ingredients used, once a particular mixture has taken hold, the chametz process can accelerate even more quickly. Egg can be a problematic ingredient in this respect. Accordingly, Ashkenazi practice developed to avoid egg Matzah other than in extenuating circumstances such as for somebody who cannot eat normal Matzah. Egg matzah is not Chametz per se.

## When is eating of Matzah required?

The Mitzvah (requirement) to eat Matzah is only at the Seder. Shabbat and other Yom Tov meals that would otherwise require Challot (breads), during Pesach require Matzah instead. The prohibition of Chametz however applies throughout Pesach.

## I have friends who eat rice and beans ("kitniyot") on Pesach and say it is because these are not Chametz. Why should I not eat these foods on Pesach?

These foods are not Chametz. Around 1,000 years ago in the Ashkenazi world, rice and beans were forbidden for Pesach as real Chametz was often found amongst them since they were grown and sown along with real Chametz grain.

They were also ground up and the flour used for baking so could easily be mistaken for regular bread.

Potato flour is nonetheless permitted since Sir Walter Raleigh did not bring potatoes to Northern Europe until the sixteenth century and accordingly potatoes were never included in the ban. Definitions of kitniyot varied in different places. Aspects of this stricture were even adopted in some Sephardi communities as well whilst on the other hand, in France, even Ashkenazim eat haricots verts (green beans) on Pesach.

## What is the search for Chametz on the night before Pesach? How can I make it seem real if I have already completed my Pesach cleaning?

Since we eat Chametz until shortly before Pesach, we double check that we have put away or disposed of all Chametz foods or drinks in our home through the search for Chametz, even though this activity is not cleaning per se. It is a last chance to check that our homes are ready for Pesach, in case we have forgotten anything; no more than a cursory search is required. Any Chametz which you have sold but remains in your house should be placed in a designated, sealed/taped up location which you will not access on Pesach. The morning after the search, destroy any remaining Chametz which has not been sold, tangibly demonstrating how we have removed the lessons of Chametz from ourselves and from our homes.

## What is Shemura Matzah and how is it different from normal matzah? Do I need to buy it?

Yes, however it is only needed for the Seder. Unlike regular Matzah, it is supervised from the earliest stages of cutting the wheat, before any mixing of flour and water, to ensure that the wheat does not get wet. Even rain falling on the cut wheat would make the flour produced unsuitable for Matzah. The wheat for Shemura Matzah must be cut by a Jew, although a farmer normally assists the Rabbi who is operating the combine harvester!

## How should I prepare my kitchen for Pesach?

See the guidance provided on the London Beth Din Kashrut division's web pages and the You&Us website. More detailed guidance is beyond our word limit here but I would emphasise that you should not turn yourself into a nervous wreck.

## Do I need to make any Pesach preparations at my place of work?

As noted above, you cannot own Chametz on Pesach so you must clear out Chametz from your personal work space. Any Chametz at work you wish to keep should be included in your sale of Chametz. Only your own personal Chametz needs to be attended to. Chametz at work that belongs to your non-Jewish employer or other members of staff can remain as is.

## Do I need to put all of my chametz utensils in a secure place outside of my kitchen?

No, these can remain in the kitchen as long as they are stowed securely in clearly marked cupboards and will not be used on Pesach.

## What should I do if I cannot afford new utensils for Pesach?

As noted above, Pesach does require extra costs and we all need to budget accordingly. Some Chametz utensils can be "kashered" under rabbinic supervision (speak to your local rabbi for guidance). Otherwise, you can buy cheap Pesach utensils or use disposables, preferably Pesach friendly bio-degradable ones.

## Can I use my normal drinking glasses on Pesach?

No, even though plain glass can normally be used for both meat and milk, as glass does not absorb, we are, nonetheless, extra stringent for Pesach.

## What is "selling Chametz" and why should I do this?

As noted above, Chametz cannot be owned over Pesach. Nullification of Chametz only applies to Chametz one never intends to use again and as such nullification does not work if you will use the Chametz after Pesach. Accordingly, a sale is required to make sure that you do not own Chametz over Pesach. It is important to emphasise that the sale is legally valid in Jewish law and is not legal fiction.

## Do I need to sell any Chametz I own in a business context?

Yes, include that Chametz in the sale of your home Chametz. If your business is trading in Chametz, please contact the London Beth Din for specific advice which is beyond the scope of this article.

## If I go away for Pesach not returning until after Pesach, do I need to clean my house?

No. Instead, you can include your house in the sale of Chametz, making provision at the time of the sale that the non Jew who purchases your Chametz also gains a rental of your home for the duration of Pesach. As with any sale of Chametz, this sale should be done through your rabbi, using the standard terms.

## Is the sale different if I am outside of the UK for Pesach?

Yes. When you contact your rabbi to arrange the sale, tell him where you will be for Pesach so that he sells your Chametz in the UK before it is Pesach in the country you are visiting and does not immediately reacquire Chametz on your behalf once Pesach has ended in the UK, should you be in a time zone behind that of the UK.

## I have seen people who avoid putting matzah in soup or eating "kneidlach"? Why is that? Can I eat "kneidlach"?

Some people avoid such foods, which are called "gebroks" in Yiddish or "Matzah Sheruya" in Hebrew, due to a concern that there may be unkneaded flour in the Matzah which would rise upon contact with water. However, most rabbis are of the view that once a Matzah has been baked it can no longer become Chametz. Each person should follow his own family's custom in this respect.

## If I go to Israel, what should I do for the second days of Yom Tov? Why does Israel only have one day of Yom Tov?

Keeping two days of Yom Tov in the Diaspora is a practice that has existed since Talmudic times due to an uncertainty in those times as to the correct date of Yom Tov. In those days, the calendar was fixed on a monthly basis by the Rabbinic court in Jerusalem and far flung Diaspora communities were concerned that they might not receive notification in good enough time. The Talmud notes that two days remained the Diaspora practice even after our present calendar cycle was instituted. Conventional halachic opinion holds, in the main, that a Diaspora Jew who goes to Israel for Yom Tov must follow the practice of the Diaspora. If you own a property in Israel and are there for each Yom Tov, there is halachic scope to allow you to keep one day on Yom Tov in Israel. This area of halacha is a good example of how halacha can be highly nuanced and answers can vary according to the facts of individual circumstances.

## What is your role and the role of the London Beth Din in helping the United Synagogue prepare for Pesach?

The Beth Din has a myriad of roles. Through the Kashrut Department it is involved in the certification of hundreds of ingredients manufactured worldwide as kosher for Pesach. It also deals with Pesach queries from all United Synagogues, other synagogues and the general public. Our work for Pesach starts each summer when we cut the wheat, as noted above.

## Who can we speak to if we have any further questions about Pesach?

Speak to your local Rabbi in the first instance or contact the London Beth Din via L&L@theus.org.uk

# UNDERSTANDING
# THE PRAYERS

# Pesach Amida Prayers
## Rabbi Anthony Knopf, Community Director, Hampstead Garden Suburb United Synagogue

### Introduction

Many of the berachot that we say as part of the Pesach Amida are the same as those recited three times a day. But what special significance do these particular prayers have for the festival of Pesach? And when we recite prayers which are specific to festivals or to Pesach itself, what are the underlying themes of these passages? What can they tell us about the meaning that the festivals communicate to us in our lives?

The festival Amida, like that of Shabbat, consists of seven blessings. Though the first three and final three blessings are identical to those recited in the Shabbat and weekday Amida, their themes assume a particular resonance on the festival of Pesach. The central section of the Amida is specific to the festivals and expresses their meaning and importance in Jewish life and thought. The table below lists each of the blessings and a summary of their respective meanings, divided into the three sections of the Amida:

|  | *Blessing* | *Theme* |
|---|---|---|
| Section 1 | 1. Magen Avraham | God's relationship and covenant with the patriarchs |
|  | 2.Mechayei Hameitim | Divine might |
|  | 3. HaEil Hakadosh | The holiness of God and the Jewish People |
| Section 2 | 4. Mekadeish Yisrael Vehazemanim | The Jews as chosen people: the festivals and our aspiration that they are observed in the optimum manner |
| Section 3 | 5. Retzei | The Temple Service |
|  | 6. Modim | Thanksgiving |
|  | 7. Shalom | Peace |

**The Themes of the Regular Festival Amida in greater detail**

## Blessing 1 – Magen Avraham (God's Relationship and Covenant with the Patriarchs)

As Moses stands at the 'burning bush', God reveals Himself as 'the God of your father, the God of Abraham, the God of Isaac and the God of Jacob'. On Pesach, the festival on which we celebrate the redemption which resulted from that encounter, we sense the poignancy in addressing ourselves to God in the very same context and terminology. Every Jewish individual is bound, not only to the Jews of the current generation, but also to his forebears, stretching back to the covenant between God and the patriarchs.

## Blessing 2 – Mechayei Hameitim (Divine Might)

This blessing, focusing on the strength of God, is evocative of God's redemption of the Israelites 'with a strong hand and an outstretched arm'. Through their witnessing of the 10 plagues and the splitting of the sea, the Israelites came to view God not only as Creator, but also as the One who manifests His powerful influence through history.

## Blessing 3 – Ha'Eil Hakadosh (The Holiness of God and the Jewish People)

When we use the word 'kadosh' (holy) in relation to God, we affirm our belief that He is not a part of nature but is, rather, above nature as its Creator. The Egyptians saw the presence of their gods in nature. For example, the Egyptian diety Ra was identified primarily with the midday sun. At Pesach, we remember that we were brought out of Egypt to become a people who related to God in a radically different manner. God is seen, not as part of the unchanging rhythm of nature, but as One who reveals a historical mission to His People. But what is that mission? That is the topic of the next section.

## Blessing 4 – Mekadeish Yisrael Vehazmanim (Who sanctifies Israel and the festive seasons)

### Ata Vechartanu (The Jews As the Chosen People)

What do we mean when we declare in our prayers that the Jews are the people chosen by God?

According to many Jewish thinkers, the Jews are the nation whose history is to bear witness to the Divine presence in the human arena.

The Pesach story draws our attention to this remarkable role of the Jewish People in at least two respects. First, the Pesach narrative contextualises the extraordinary survival and impact of the Jewish People throughout history. At the beginning of the story, the Hebrews are a group of slaves, oppressed by an indomitable power. Any claim at the time that it would be the slaves and not the mighty empire that would survive and change the moral landscape of the world would have been met with complete incredulity. The lowly origins of the Jewish People amplify our appreciation of the miracle of Jewish survival.

Second, through the Exodus story, God communicated to the world the dream for freedom from oppression. In liberating this group of undistinguished and persecuted slaves from their mighty oppressors, the message was communicated that God loves those whom the world despises and that human dignity is not dependent upon power and privilege. The echoes of this message reverberated millennia later as the movements led by the black Americans, the American liberation theologians and Nelson Mandela applied the Biblical teaching to their own plight. As the essayist, Heinrich Heine[1], once wrote, 'Since the Exodus, freedom has always spoken with a Hebrew accent'.

### Vatitein lanu (The Festivals)

On Pesach, we are called upon to celebrate with gladness and joy. Here, we give thanks to God for this opportunity. The festival is described with the Biblical term 'mikra kodesh' or 'holy assembly'. The Biblical commentator, Nachmanides[2], explains that this term refers to the call for Jews to gather together in shul on the Chagim (festivals) to sanctify the festival through the recital of the special Yom Tov prayers.

### Eloheinu Ve'Elohei Avoteinu (Our Aspiration for a Fully Redeemed World).

Having declared our gratitude for the current celebration of Pesach, we now pray that God should grant us a full redemption. The festival of Pesach is not only of historical interest but, to this day, it informs our longings for a better world. On this festival, we yearn for the Messianic time when 'the earth shall be full of the knowledge of the LORD, as the waters cover the sea'[3]. Pesach is not only the celebration of the redemption from Egypt, but also part of the process towards our future redemption. That is why the bulk of the Haftarah of the eighth day of Pesach speaks of the future messianic redemption and why our Pesach Seder ends with the declaration: 'Next Year in Jerusalem '.

### Vehasi'einu (Bestow upon us)

The final paragraph of the central portion concludes with a blessing to God 'Who sanctifies [the People of] Israel and the festive seasons'. As noted in the Talmud, this differs from the beracha (blessing) on Shabbat which we conclude with the words 'Who sanctifies Shabbat', with no mention made of the sanctification of Israel[4]. The Talmud explains that whereas the Shabbat occurs on a Divinely ordained timetable and therefore is "sanctified by God", the festivals' timings depend in part upon the Jewish People and therefore the sanctification of the festivals is transmitted through the Jewish People. This is because it is the Jewish People – more specifically, the Rabbinic Court – who were charged with the responsibility of regulating the calendar. This responsibility continued until the Romans forcibly dissolved those Rabbinic Courts with the seniority and standing to regulate the calendar. Subsequently, Jewish people moved to the fixed calendar that we use today. When exactly our calendar was fixed is a matter of dispute[5].

1       1797-1856.
2       Rabbi Moshe ben Nachman, 1194-1270, known by the acronym "Ramban".
3       Isaiah 11:9.
4       This is discussed in the Talmud, Beitzah 17a.
5       See the writings of Rabbi Professor Sacha Stern.

## Blessing 5 - Retzei (The Temple Service)

With the 'Retzei' blessing, we begin the first of the final three berachot of the Amida.

The theme of 'Retzei' is the restoration of the Temple service. Although part of the daily prayer service, this blessing also has particular relevance to the festivals. It is on the festivals that the Jews were commanded to make a pilgrimage to the Temple to bring offerings. Indeed, it is for this reason that Pesach, Shavuot and Sukkot are referred to as the Shalosh Regalim, the "Three Foot Festivals". Without the rebuilding of the Temple we are unable to fulfil the true essence of the festival.

## Blessing 6 - Modim (Thanksgiving)

Through the Exodus, God's goodness and love became overwhelmingly evident to the Israelites. They had not done anything to deserve this miraculous release. Freedom had come to them as an act of sheer unmerited love. We are not surprised to find them exclaiming: 'Who is like you among the gods, O God?'[6].

This provides the basis for the thanksgiving we express in the Modim prayer. Moreover, on Pesach, the festival on which our Exodus heritage is communicated to the next generation, we express our thanks for the privilege of inheriting a wonderful way of life and set of values. This blessing makes reference to 'al nisecha' (all Your miracles) which is reminiscent of all of the miracles of Pesach.

## Blessing 7 - Shalom (Peace)

In the Shacharit morning service, this blessing begins with the words 'Sim Shalom' ('grant peace').

In it, all our prayers are condensed in the wish to be blessed with the Divine countenance. However we may marvel at the privilege of national freedom celebrated at Pesach, we are reminded that the spiritual experience lies at the heart of Judaism.

In the Mincha afternoon and Maariv evening services, the blessing begins with 'Shalom Rav' ('abundant peace'). This is a request for abundant peace in face of the unknown dangers of the impending darkness. On Pesach, the rabbis instruct us to 'start with the shame and conclude with the praise'[7]. Life includes many trials and tribulations but the Exodus story provides us with a model of hope for better times.

### The Special Themes of the Mussaf Amida

As on Shabbat, the festival liturgy contains a Mussaf service. This service differs significantly in its role and content and will require a separate discussion as set out below.

### Umipnei Chata'einu (But Because of Our Sins)

The central section of the Mussaf Amida focuses on the sacrifices which were offered in the Temple and specific mention is made of those offered on Pesach.

In this section, we pray for the revelation of God's great glory. Although such supplications are also included in the Mussaf Amida of Shabbat and the New

---

6     Shemot/Exodus 15:11.
7     See BT Pesachim 116a.

Month, they are expressed with much greater intensity in the festival Mussaf Amida. The festive mood and appreciation of our former redemption makes us all the more aware of the sad depths to which humanity is wont to fall as illustrated by the world still waiting for the fulfilment of the Biblical prophecies of the future redemption.

## Tal

The repetition of the Mussaf Amida on the second day of Pesach includes a special prayer for dew, called "Tefilat Tal". Indeed, this prayer marks the beginning of the season in which we pray for dew. This is based on the idea that there is a consistency between the renewal of the Jewish People at the redemption and the rejuvenation of nature.

## Birkat Kohanim (The Priestly Blessing)

Many of us are used to the 'Duchanning' service in which all the Kohanim ascend the ark and bless the community. But, whilst this blessing is recited daily in most parts of Israel, in the Diaspora it is only recited at Mussaf on festivals. Why? The reason is that a Kohen should be in a state of joy when giving a blessing and, only on these Yom Tov days of happiness, can we be confident that he will truly capture the joyous mood of the heart.

And why do the Kohanim remove their shoes before the blessing? This is to emphasise the sacred character of the blessing and to remind us of God's instruction to Moses to remove his shoes at the burning bush.

Before the Kohanim begin, the prayer leader calls out "Kohanim" in order to summon them to bless the congregation. The prayer leader then dictates the blessing to the Kohanim word by word. The congregation answers "Amen" after each of the three stages of the blessings. According to Rabbi Samson Raphael Hirsch[8], the reason for this is to convey the fact that the priests are merely passive instruments, officials of the people who are permitted to bless their congregation only after they have been called upon to do so. The Kohen (singular of Kohanim) himself is not the source and giver of the blessing.

The priestly blessing is a blessing of love. It is interesting that this is the only blessing over a mitzvah (commandment) which concludes with the word 'b'ahava' (with love). This underscores the necessity for the blessing to be conveyed wholeheartedly.

## Conclusion

The Jewish liturgy has a timeless quality. Though much of the content of the Shabbat, Festival and Weekday Amida is identical, the words acquire a specific resonance at different times of the year. We pray every day for the rebuilding the Temple but, on Pesach, the same prayer expresses our desire to stand together in the Temple to offer the Pascal Sacrifice. We pray each day for peace, but on Pesach, that peace speaks of an ultimate redemption an everlasting peace.

Our Chagim (festivals) are the highlights of our Jewish year. They are designed to boost our Jewish lifestyle and to stand apart from our routine in order to enhance not only the Chagim themselves, but our daily routine as well.

---

8        A leading German rabbi (1808-1888) whose  most prominent post was in Frankfurt.

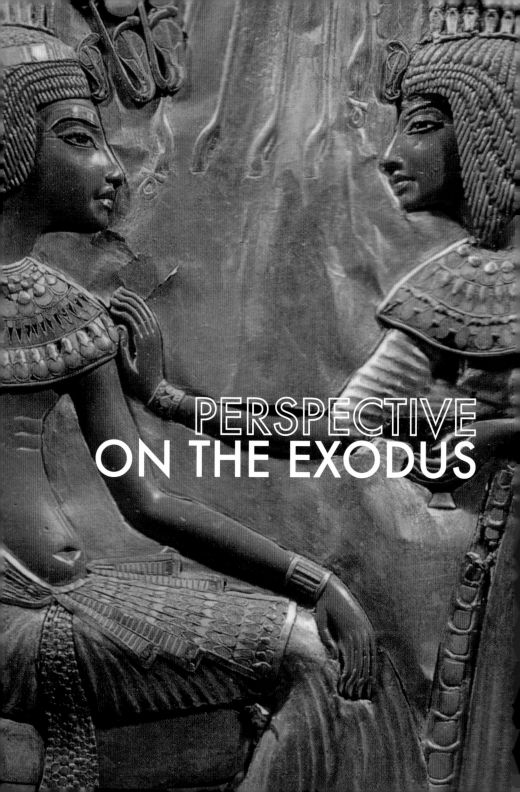

# PERSPECTIVE
# ON THE EXODUS

# Slaves, plagues and pharaonic knaves, plus a surprisingly useful idol: "An Egyptological perspective on the Exodus"

*Rabbi Arye Forta is a noted author and speaker. He currently runs a series of Tanach Tours at the British Museum.*

'We were slaves to Pharaoh in Egypt and God our God took us out from there with a strong hand and an outstretched arm'. With these words we start our explanation of the Seder celebration. Yet even as we read them, encapsulating, as they do, the essence of Pesach, we recognise that their seeming simplicity belies a lengthy and complex process - the obduracy of a divine king (as seen by his subjects), ten devastating plagues and the drowning of an army –before freedom was finally won. Today, aided by information gleaned from Egyptology, we can appreciate just how complex that process really was.

As a rule, we tend to think of the plagues either as a well deserved punishment for years of brutal oppression or a demonstration of God's awesome power. They are, of course, both. But they are also more than that. Time and again, Moses conveys God's message – the next plague will come so that 'with this you shall know that I am God' (Shemot/Exodus 7: 17); 'in order that you may know that I am God' (ib. 8:18); 'so that you should know that there is none like Me...' (ib. 9: 14). The plagues were essentially an educational programme - God's attempt to make the Egyptians realise that the gods they worshipped were not gods at all and that they should recognise that He alone is God.

From the numerous texts that have come down to us from ancient times, we know that the Egyptians saw their world in terms of dualities. The dualities of the physical environment - fertile mud plane/arid desert; Upper Egypt/ Lower Egypt - were mirrored in human dualities such as the kings' double title 'nesu bity'. Both terms mean 'king', the former referring to his sacral office (he was high priest of all the gods) the latter to his secular roles. (Contrary to popular belief, 'Pharaoh' does not mean king).

One of the most significant dualities was the ongoing interplay of *maat* (truth/order) and *isfet* (falsehood/chaos). Ultimately, it was down to the king to maintain and, if necessary restore, *maat*. The encroachment of *isfet* would reflect on the king's ability to perform his divinely appointed task. We should bear this in mind when looking at Pharaoh's reaction to the plagues.

The Torah does not dwell on the details of the slavery, but we know from numerous Midrashim (early rabbinic commentaries on the Torah) that it was brutal. However, the Torah does tell us that our ancestors built the two eastern delta cities of Pitom. (Pi Atum - House of [the god] Atum) and Ramses (Per Ramesse 'a nakhtu - House of Ramesses, Great of Victories). The latter was Ramesses II's new capital, thus allowing us to identify the otherwise unnamed Pharaoh (not with total certainty, admittedly, but he is the only one who fits the details the Torah gives us and this is the identification assumed here). The city took twenty years of unceasing labour to build.

After 67 years on the throne, Ramesses died, leaving his thirteenth son and successor, Merenptah (who we will also refer to interchangeably as "Pharaoh"), to face the wrath of the God of Israel. 'After these many days the King of Egypt died', ibid 2:23, (where the phrase 'many days' is a euphemism for an exceptionally long time) probably refers to the length of Ramesses' reign.

Within months of Merenptah coming to the throne, Moses and Aaron were in Egypt trying to negotiate the freeing of the slaves and performing various signs in Merenptah's presence. However, since the magicians (who, according to some commentaries, were not 'magicians' at all but illusionists) seemed able to do similar things, the Pharaoh remained unimpressed. Convinced that only lazy slaves dream of freedom, he decided to make them work harder. From now on the Israelite brick makers would have to find their own straw (an essential binding agent of mud bricks) while still producing the same daily quota (ibid 5: 6-12). Merenptah needed more forceful persuasion. It was time to start the plagues.

First to be smitten was the Nile. Each summer, torrential rain in what is today Ethiopia, sent turbulent waters surging northwards causing the Nile to overflow its banks. In the autumn, when the flood waters receded, they left a deposit of mineral rich mud on the river banks producing some of the most fertile soil in the ancient Near East. The Egyptians, not knowing the source of the flood waters and their soil-enriching mud, assumed it was the beneficence of the Nile god.

It is not difficult to imagine how much disruption and consternation was caused when what was once Egypt's source of sustenance was now a thousand mile long pool of blood, reeking with the stench of dead fish. However, Merenptah's magicians again seemed able to reproduce the same effect and the Pharaoh shrugged it off (ibid 7: 23).

The second plague was frogs. Moses warned Pharaoh in graphic detail what to expect –'the frogs will swarm in the river and they will rise and go into your houses, into your bedrooms and your beds…..into your ovens and kneading basins' (ibid 7: 28). Though not life-threatening, they would become an intolerable nuisance throughout Egypt.

But there was a deeper significance; and if the full import of the plague is lost on us it would have been painfully clear to the Egyptians. They thought of many of their gods as being associated with animals. Among their many deities was one always depicted as a woman with a frog's head. She was thought to be present at each birth; blowing the breath of life into the new born baby's nostrils and making the child live. The plague's message was clear – this goddess who is so important to you because she gives you life is really no god at all. She is a frog, nothing more, and the God of Israel is using them against you.

Again, the Egyptian sorcerers produced a similar result, but this time Merenptah was worried. It suddenly dawned on him that the plague of blood had not been a one-off – it looked as though there was more to come. As king he had to maintain *maat*; if he was seen to allow *isfet* to go unchecked his relationship with his gods was in jeopardy. He had no option but to call on Moses' help (ibid 8: 4).

Lice followed. This time it showed the impotence of the magicians (ibid 8: 14) and, by implication, (since most would have been priests of various deities) of the gods they served. We are not told what Pharaoh's response was. But from the

'plague of blood'

next plague on, he consistently called for Moses to remove what must have been a truly terrifying experience throughout Egypt. And, of course, each successive plague was another outbreak of *isfet* – showing the king increasingly incapable of getting the situation under control.

The fourth plague, Arov, which encompassed wild animals roaming free and causing havoc (ibid 8: 20), was a watershed in the educational programme. As mentioned earlier, the Egyptians thought of almost all their gods as being associated with animals. Statues and tomb painting depict male and female gods either as animals plain and simple, as humans with animal heads or as animals with human heads (which we call a sphinx). Arov, whereby the very animals the Egyptians worshipped were being used against them, was the ultimate demonstration that these were no gods at all.

By now Pharaoh is so desperate that he not only agreed to let the Israelites go free, he even asked Moses to pray for him (ibid verse 24).

The next few plagues highlighted the impotence of the priests who served the gods (ibid 9: 11) and, more specifically, the gods of the harvest. Then we come to the ninth plague - darkness. It is difficult for us today to visualise just how important a god the sun was for the ancient Egyptians. It was the source of light and warmth, and its regular setting in the west and rising again each morning made it a powerful symbol of rebirth after death. The Egyptians, following the sun's daily journey, buried their dead on the west bank of the Nile in expectation of that same rebirth. So too, each king bore the title sa Re, son of the sun god, with whom he expected to be reunited after death. The ninth plague, wherein the sun was trying to make the world bright but the God of Israel had made it dark (ibid 10: 22), was a direct repudiation of the sun's divinity.

*Merenptah, probably the Pharaoh with whom Moses negotiated*

By now, apart from a slight change of heart on the part of some Egyptians (ibid 9: 20) it began to look as though the educational programme had failed. They were not going to abandon their gods. Nonetheless, the Israelites had to be freed. It was time to send a plague so devastating that Merenptah would have no choice but to let them go.

Now God continued to show the impotence of Egypt's gods while, at the same time, giving the Israelites a mitzvah (commandment) that demanded immense courage. Among the Egyptians' many gods, only a select few were known as 'great gods'. The sheep was one of them. There is a sculpture in the British

Museum that shows the king, minuscule compared to the giant sheep above him, cradled between its paws. Pharaoh, the most powerful man in the world of his day, needed the protection of the sheep god! The Israelites were commanded to take this hugely important Egyptian deity, keep it tied up for four days and then slaughter it (ibid 12: 3-6).

The killing of all first-born Egyptian sons had the desired effect. It could hardly have been otherwise. Merenptah, considering himself the first-born of the sun god (in fact he was his father's thirteenth son and his mother's third), feared for his own life. Obdurate from the start, he now wanted the Israelites out as soon as possible.

It is impossible to imagine the Israelites' feelings as they left Egypt – relief, euphoria, hope, uncertainty of what the future might bring. Probably a mixture of all of these and more besides. At the same time, they must have been aware that there was always the possibility of Pharaoh coming after them to haul them back into slavery. Then, only three days after leaving Egypt behind them, a curious event took place – an event that both tested Israel's faith to the limit as well as showing decisively that God's attempt to re-educate the Egyptians was over. The Israelites were commanded to turn back the way they had come and make camp near the desert shrine of Baal Tzefon (ibid 14: 1-3)!

The significance of Baal Tzefon needs to be understood. Some four hundred years before the exodus, Egypt had been invaded by Asiatic hordes known to us as the Hyksos. They had settled in Lower Egypt where they had ruled for about a century. It was commonplace in the ancient world that when groups of people migrated and settled in a new land they would take with them their household goods, their livestock and also their gods. Sooner or later, the incoming gods would he identified with the native gods. So it was that, gradually, the Hyksos' storm god, bearing the Semitic name Baal (called in the Torah, Baal Tzefon – Baal of the North), became identified with the Egyptians' own storm god. Long after the Hyksos had been driven out, the Egyptian and Semitic names were still being used as alternative forms of address for this deity.

Merenptah's family hailed from the northern city of Nubt (modern Magada) which was regarded as the home of the storm god. To them, he was their patron god. So when the Israelites camped by his desert shrine Pharaoh assumed that, whereas his gods had failed him, his own personal god (aka Baal Tzefon) was still working for him against the god of Israel (cf. 3rd Rashi on Shemot/Exodus 14:2) and would help him bring them back as slaves. Merenptah took the bait. The result was the drowning of his host in the Sea of Reeds, leaving the Israelites completely free.

But there is a curious twist to the tale. Pharaoh had been spared from drowning with his army so that he could return to Egypt and testify to the might of God. What he did instead really highlights how far he was from recognising God.

Even after the departure of his slaves, Merenptah's troubles were far from over. In the fifth year of his reign, Egypt was invaded by Libyan hordes from the west. Pharaoh repulsed them temporarily and then set out on a military campaign in Canaan. On his return, he had a victory stele carved proclaiming his triumphs. Among the peoples he claims to have defeated is Israel – it is the earliest mention of Israel in any Egyptian text known so far. In a few carefully carved hieroglyphs, Merenptah boasts, 'Israel is laid waste, his seed is no more'.

How are we to understand this? Curiously, Merenptah gives himself away not by what he writes, but by what he leaves out. Recounting his victory over Ashkelon, Gezer and Yenoam, each of these is supplied with a hieroglyph denoting a territory (it looks like three hills). The name Israel is not, indicating that the Israelites are not in a settled territory (in fact they would have been miles away somewhere on their forty year trek through the desert). But Merenptah is trying to cover his tracks. Everyone knows that he set out in pursuit of the Israelites and that he came back empty handed. With this inscription he is, in effect, saying, "No, I've not brought the Israelites, back; but don't worry, I've destroyed them!" And who would know otherwise?

Within fifty years of Merenptah's death, Egypt began a centuries-long decline into oblivion. First she was conquered by the Libyans whom Merenptah had fought to keep at bay. Then, apart from brief interludes of native resurgence, she was conquered by Nubians, Assyrians, Persians, and Macedonians. Finally, some twelve hundred years after the exodus, Egypt became one more province of the Roman Empire and the Kingdom of the Pharaohs was no more. And we are still here to celebrate our Seder.

The name Iskelon (Ashkelon) on Merenptah's stele.

The three hills symbol in the lower right corner indicates a territory he claims to have conquered.

The name Israer (Israel) as it appears on the stele.

The three vertical lines under the man and women indicate the plural, telling us to read 'men and women', i.e. a group of people; note the absence of the three hills.

*For details of Rabbi Forta's Tanach tours at the British Museum, email tours@forta.com or visit www.livingjewishhistory.com*

# CARING/CHESED SECTION

כָּל דִּכְפִין יֵיתֵי וְיֵכוֹל , כָּל דִּצְרִיךְ יֵיתֵי וְיִפְסַח

## "Kol dichfin yeitei v'yeichol, kol ditztrich yetei ve'yifsach"

## Let anyone who is hungry, come and eat. Let anyone who is in need, come and celebrate Pesach

*Rabbi Andrew Shaw*

One reason why Seder night has lived on while other traditions have fallen by the wayside, is the fact that it takes place in the home, not in the shul.

At the start of our Seder we call out the quote above, "All who are needy let them come and eat". Do we mean it? At that point in time we are already sitting round the table. No one needy is going to come in at that stage of the proceedings. What can that line mean for us today?

Many years ago, I was in Israel with a group of teenagers. I took them to Yad Vashem. There is a film there about the history of Jewish life in Europe. It tells of life in the poor Jewish shtetls and ghettos but nevertheless in every one there was a soup kitchen, a free lending society and a whole host of charitable organisations. During this part one of the teenagers turned to me and said "The Jewish community was so poor. How could people give so much charity?" he asked. "Why do you think?" I said. His answer was profoundly beautiful, "I guess they wouldn't have been a community otherwise". Somehow Jews know that community is vital, and a community without welfare is not a community. Even when we could hardly feed ourselves we still tried to feed others. Mi ke'amcha yisrael?– Who is like the Jewish Nation?

That has always characterised a Jewish community; caring for others less fortunate than ourselves.

In this third section of the Guide we turn to various areas of 'caring'. Looking after people in hospital over Pesach, ways you can help the world around you and how we look after students who may be away from home on Pesach.

The Seder begins with a message of caring for people. Let us live that message at Pesach and beyond, doing our best to ensure that nobody feels alone.

PESACH
IN HOSPITAL

# Pesach in Hospital
### by Rabbi Meir Salasnik, Rabbi of Bushey United Synagogue and senior Jewish Hospital Chaplain

Perhaps the first thing that needs to be mentioned in regard to being in hospital, whether during Pesach or at any other time of the year, is that in most hospitals, there is no way that the Jewish Chaplain or visitor will know that a Jewish patient is in hospital, unless either the patient, a relative or a friend initiates contact. Gone are the days when the chaplain of any faith could arrive at the hospital information desk and receive a list of patients of his or her faith who are in that hospital. Legislation about data protection has led to hospitals not divulging such information, and while they accept that a patient may require the services of a visitor of their faith, they consider it is up to the patient to decide whether he or she wishes to ask for the services of the visitor of their faith connected to the hospital or even a person of another faith.

One of the most unusual hospital visits I have made was when an elderly Greek Christian lady, whose son had suffered an accident which rendered him brain dead, asked for a Rabbi to visit and recite prayers before he passed away.

Nonetheless, there are a few hospitals which accept that it is appropriate to share information with faith visitors. However, apart from the fact that they are in the minority, there is no guarantee that the ward clerk will enter information regarding faith on the database. So, there is no substitute for the patient or his or her representative making the call to their Rabbi, the hospital visiting chaplain or visitor, or to the full-time chaplain to request that he or she initiates a Jewish visit.

## PESACH MEALS IN HOSPITAL

In terms of Pesach requirements, Hospital Kosher Meals Service, (HKMS) www.hkms.org.uk supplies hospitals with Kosher for Passover lunches and suppers. Here is the notice HKMS sends to synagogues for their notice boards:

## PESACH MEALS

**WE WILL BE SUPPLYING HOSPITALS IN THE LONDON AREA WITH SUPERVISED KOSHER FOR PESACH MEALS. IF YOU ARE MAKING USE OF THIS SERVICE DURING THE PESACH PERIOD, PLEASE NOTE THE FOLLOWING:-**

**THE MEALS, SOUPS AND DESSERTS YOU RECEIVE MUST EACH HAVE A YELLOW LABEL CLEARLY MARKED "KOSHER FOR PASSOVER". HOSPITALS HAVE THE OPTION OF PURCHASING PASSOVER BREAKFASTS.**

The experience of HKMS is that few hospitals take up the opportunity of the Kosher for Passover breakfast which contains a small pack of matzos, fruit juice, yoghurt, a soft cheese portion and jam, tea, coffee and lemon juice sachets. The reluctance is not for reasons of cost, but because in most hospitals, breakfast is supplied by the individual ward and not by the hospital kitchen.

This means that many patients would be reliant on their family for their Pesach breakfast.

HKMS does not supply anything for the Seder, which means that in terms of wine, Matzah, Maror and Charoset, the patient is reliant on family or friends.

With reference to the rest of the year, in recent months, it has been possible in a couple of hospitals, Homerton and Royal Free, to have traditional kosher Shabbat meals.

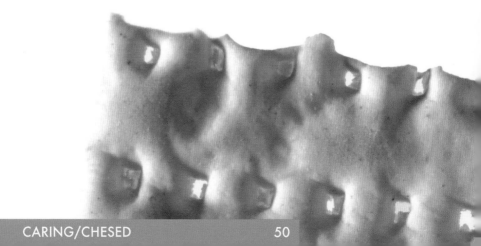

## PESACH MEALS FOR RELATIVES

Ezra U'Marpeh, based in North London, has pioneered assistance for relatives staying with patients over Shabbat. They have initiated Shabbat rooms in Homerton, Barnet, Great Ormond Street, Royal Free and Royal London Hospitals, and a Shabbat cupboard in University College Hospitals. Prior to Pesach, they kasher and prepare these rooms and cupboards for Pesach use. They plan to have facilities to enable relatives to celebrate the Seder. They can be contacted at 020 8211 7999 or 07976 826846.

## MEDICATION

Regarding medication for Pesach, the website of the Kashrut department of the London Beth Din will have information at www.kosher.org.uk/passover.htm. As a general rule of thumb, if a person is seriously ill and the most effective medication for that person is not kosher or not kosher for Pesach, the medication should be taken. If there is a kosher or kosher for Pesach alternative that is as good, that kosher alternative should be taken.

## SEDER

What part of the Haggadah is required? There are hospital patients who are well enough to recite the whole of the Haggadah and others who will be unable to recite anything. Some may only be able to recite a small amount of the Haggadah. If so, Avadim Hayinu, which is the paragraph following Mah Nishtanah, and the three items which Rabban Gamliel considered obligatory, namely the explanations for Pesach, Matzah and Maror, are among the most essential.

The timing of the Seder can be difficult for some, as the appropriate time is to start after nightfall, although in an emergency one can start about a quarter of an hour after sunset. Check these times with your local rabbi.

**If you have any further questions please do contact me via the US Living & Learning department at** L&L@theus.org.uk

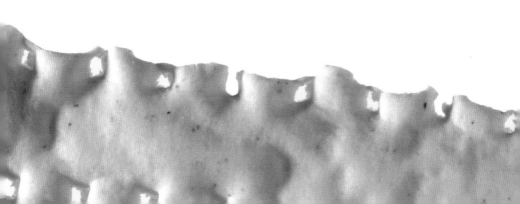

GIVING STRENGTH
TO ALL JEWISH
STUDENTS

# 30 days before Pesach...

*Rabbi Daniel and Hannah Braune Friedman are Jewish Chaplains for Oxford and Oxford Brookes Universities.*

There is a custom to start studying the laws of Pesach immediately after the Purim Seudah (festive meal). This follows the Talmud[1] which tells one to review the Pesach laws 30 days before the festival starts. In Chaplaincy, that would be a far too late! We had our first official chat about how we could support students with the many different aspects and unique challenges that Pesach presents just after Tu B'shevat, three months early! The challenges include cleaning, selling Chametz, "kashering" (preparing utensils for Pesach), preparing the Seder and catering. Before every festival we send information to students about halachot (laws), meals and chesed (kindness) and what programmes and hospitality we are offering. When preparing for Pesach, the first challenge is to assess which students will actually be staying in Oxford.

While we do our best to create a "home away from home" for them during their time at University, most students choose to go home for Pesach but even they still have many practical questions for us. For example, what does one do about food they might be leaving behind as how does one sell Chametz? Students also ask about what they could do to enhance their Pesach experience at home.

There are always a significant number of graduate students and foreign students who remain on campus in between terms. In addition this year, Oxford Brookes is in session during Pesach. Those who stay need support and guidance about how best to manage the various issues that Pesach throws up. One common question is how to avoid Chametz when sharing a flat or house with somebody who is not Jewish. We also have a lot of students with us for Seder. Last year, 30 joined us for Seder with many more enjoying hospitality during Chol Hamoed (the middle days) and for the last days of Pesach.

Of course, food is not the only thing we are concerned about. We carefully make sure that we create the right atmosphere in our home, especially for the Seder. Designing a meaningful Seder is the "matzah and butter" of our job. It has to have the right blend of creativity and tradition, keeping the well-known sounds, tastes and aromas of Pesach whilst introducing new ideas to create a really special atmosphere reflecting the variety of students from different backgrounds. We give the students lots of opportunities to ask questions and discuss issues; we have a tradition of asking each guest to share one aspect of their lives that makes them feel constrained and one that makes them feel liberated.

Finally, we always try to make sure that all students know we are only a phonecall/email/facebook/twitter away from anything they might need.

---

1    See, for example, the Talmud in Tractate Pesachim 6a.

CARING/CHESED

SEEING
FREEDOM

# Four ways to bring more freedom to the world

### by Candice Woolfson, US Chesed Director and member of Finchley United Synagogue

"This is the bread of affliction that our fathers ate in the land of Egypt. Let all who are hungry come and eat..." ('Ha Lachma Anya', from the Pesach Haggadah).

Primo Levi was a survivor of Auschwitz. In his book, *If This is a Man*, he describes his experience there. According to Levi, the worst time of all was when the Nazis left in January 1945, fearing the Russian advance. All prisoners who could walk were taken on the brutal 'death marches'. The only people left in the camp were those who were too ill to move. For ten days they were left alone with only scraps of food and fuel. Levi describes how he worked to light a fire and bring some warmth to his fellow prisoners, many of them dying. He writes:

'When the broken window was repaired and the stove began to spread its heat, something seemed to relax in everyone, and at that moment Towarowski (a Franco-Pole of twenty-three) proposed to the others that each of them offer a slice of bread to us three who had been working. And so it was agreed.

Only a day before a similar event would have been inconceivable. The law of the Lager said: "eat your own bread, and if you can, that of your neighbour," and left no room for gratitude. It really meant that the law of the lager was dead.

It was the first human gesture that occurred amongst us. I believe that that moment can be dated as the beginning of the change by which we who had not died slowly changed from prisoners to men again.'

(Excerpted from *The Chief Rabbi's Haggadah*, Lord Sacks, Harper Collins, 2003)

This story illustrates in a very moving way how sharing food is the first act through which slaves become human beings. Someone in fear of tomorrow doesn't offer his food to others.

In Haiti, the poor often repeat this proverb: "Bondye konn bay, men li pa konn sepere" meaning "God gives but he does not share." God gives us everything we need to flourish, but it is up to us to choose to share it. This is the bread of affliction only so long as it resides in our hand, and not in the hands of others. The Chief Rabbi tells us that this is why we begin the Seder by inviting others to join us.

CARING/CHESED

We have four ideas of ways in which you can make a difference and transform the bread of affliction into the bread of freedom. Some of these ideas can be actioned before the first Seder, others after.

The first idea is our Chametz for the Homeless initiative that is being coordinated across several United Synagogue communities. Rather than throwing your Chametz away before Pesach – or selling it – why not give it away to someone who would really appreciate it? Each participating shul has a designated place where food (tins, cartons and other sealed packets) can be dropped off. We then link each community with a local homeless hostel. It's a simple project yet the goodwill generated is huge, not to mention the fact that you can enjoy your Seder in the comfort of knowing that someone else is eating because of you.

We'd love more communities to get involved. Just contact us if you can help organise a collection in your community or if you want to find out the location of your nearest food drop-off. Even after Pesach you can still set up a food drop-off point in your community and we can help you do it. Contact us if you want to get involved (see contact details at the end of the article).

> '*let all who are hungry come and eat and let all who are needy come and celebrate Pesach*'

The second idea is to invite people to your Seder. No one should spend Seder alone. Have you considered inviting two extra guests who may not have anywhere to go? Talk to your Rabbi, administrator or care co-coordinator as they may know of people in the community who might be alone at Pesach - or people who don't know how to make a Seder themselves. Ha Lachma Anya says "let all who are hungry come and eat" and also says "let all who are needy come and celebrate Pesach". Needy could refer to those who can afford the food, but are not in a position to conduct or lead a Seder themselves. And this might be where you can help.

If you are away for Pesach or can't fit in any more guests then you can always try to invite some extra guests on another Yom Tov, or for a Shabbat meal.

The third idea relates to giving food to the hungry. Meir Panim is a charity that provides meals and other critical services to Israel's poor in locations throughout the country. Every day their 14 soup kitchens hand out literally thousands of nutritious meals – free of charge. Each served with warmth and dignity.

Meir Panim is always looking for volunteers to help prepare and serve food to their appreciative diners. Next time you are in Israel why not add them onto your itinerary? With locations throughout the country, there's likely to be a Meir Panim branch not far from wherever you are planning on staying. The experience is guaranteed to enrich your trip, and perhaps even your life. Go to www.meirpanimuk.org to find out more.

And for those of you with no trips planned to Israel, why not log on to the Hunger Site website?

24,000 people die every day from hunger. Three quarters of the deaths are children under the age of 5. By visiting 'The Hunger Site' and clicking the 'Give Free Food' button, a cup of food is donated to people in need in one of over 70 countries. The food donation is paid for by a sponsor, and the cost of running the site is paid for by advertisements. If you've not heard of this site before, I know it sounds unbelievable. But there's no catch. It costs you absolutely nothing but the time it takes you to log on and click a button – and yet it feeds a hungry person. Go to www.thehungersite.com for more information.

And finally our fourth suggestion is to prepare a meal for someone who needs it. I know from my own experiences that there are times in our lives when we just don't have a minute to think about buying or preparing food to eat:

People who are sitting Shiva rely on friends, family and their community to provide them with ready-cooked meals.

New mothers find that they are suddenly busy 24-7 with hardly any time to do anything but take care of their baby.

People who are ill, housebound, or unable to go shopping or cook, often have a diet as limited as their contact with the outside world.

In many communities, people prepare Kosher ready-to-eat meals and then keep them in a communal freezer, so that when someone can't cook for themselves or their family, proper meals are instantly available.

If your shul doesn't do this, and you are someone who doesn't mind cooking, why not get involved? Contact your shul care co-coordinator to offer, or contact me to find out more.

US Chesed teaches the Jewish responsibility we have for our fellow human beings, encourages more acts of charity and kindness and inspires our community to make a difference. If you want to volunteer, either within our synagogue-based community care groups that support our members in times of need, or with our Project Chesed initiatives that reach out to the wider Jewish community, or the wider world in which we're living, please be in touch: **uschesed@theus.org.uk or 020 8343 5688.**

*Every act of goodness that we do will bring us closer to the hope with which the "Ha Lachma Anya" section of the Haggadah ends... "next year, may we all be free." Chag Sameach.*

# LOOKING INTO THE HAGGADAH

# Introduction to the Haggadah Section

*Rabbi Andrew Shaw*

The inspiration for the Haggadah stems from God's command to Moses in Shemot/Exodus 13:8, "And you shall relate [vehigadta] to your child [student/other person] on that very day saying, because of this, God acted for me when I came out of Egypt."

The Hebrew verb "vehigadta" is related to the noun "Haggadah", giving us a name for the text we use at the Seder.

Whilst the instruction for us each to relate something about the Exodus is clear, the verse does not clarify what that something is. In fact, the verse seems rather bland in stating, "because of this". My English literature A-Level teacher would not have approved of my translation, I fear!

Rabbi Moses ben Nachman (1194-1270), popularly known as "Ramban", who wrote one of the most important commentaries on the Torah, writes on our verse that the phrase "because of this" means that we must relate the Exodus story as if we had actually seen the events we are describing.

In this vein, we are delighted in this section to present reflections written by rabbis and members from a variety of United Synagogue communities on selected parts of the Haggadah.

We hope that you too will add your own insights into the Exodus and Seder evening, as Jews do every year, reliving the story and making your mark on Jewish history.

# SPLITTING
# THE MIDDLE
# MATZAH

# *Yachatz*

## *Saffron Sheridan, Megan Burack, & Rosie Ferner-Cornhouse (all Year 8 students at King Solomon High School)*

What is Yachatz? Yachatz is an introductory part of the Haggadah involving Matzah. It is the fourth stage in the Seder service. During this part of the service the middle Matzah is broken in two. Matzah is referred to as the "poor man's bread." Just as a poor man does not know when his next meal is coming, so we too place the larger piece aside for later in the Seder, in recognition of the slavery of Egypt. It is one of the many ritual acts that turn the food of the Seder into a symbol of meaning. The remaining larger part of the broken Matzah is then put aside for the Afikoman.

It is well known that the leader of the Seder hides the Afikoman. Afterwards, children get the pleasure of going to hunt for the Afikoman and are often promised a present when they return the Afikoman to the leader of the Seder before Birkat Hamazon (Grace after Meals). However, the smaller piece also represents 'the bread of affliction' which, after Yachatz, is returned to the Seder plate and eaten later in the Seder as part of the mitzvah of Matzah. At the end of the meal the bigger piece, which was hidden originally, is also eaten, as the Afikoman'.

The bottom Matzah, which remained untouched during Yachatz, will be used later in the Seder for the Hillel sandwich (the Korech) made of Matzah, Maror, and Charoset.

# Ha Lachma Anya

*Rebecca Filer, year 10 pupil at JFS and member of South Hampstead United Synagogue*

In my family, we have a tradition to buy a new and interesting Haggadah every few years and with this strange custom comes the problem of housing our rather large collection. But the best thing about this is the range of Rabbinic and modern views that are found in their pages.

I have chosen to share a few views on Ha Lachma Anya, the beginning of the narration of the Pesach story, from a selection of my family's favourite Haggadot, the first of these being the 19th century commentary of the Malbim[1] (my Dad's choice). Ha Lachma Anya says:

"This is the bread of affliction that our fathers ate in the land of Egypt.

Let all who are hungry come and eat.

Let all who are needy come and celebrate Passover.

This year we are here – next year may we be in the land of Israel.

This year we are slaves – next year may we be free"

(Translation: *The Chief Rabbi's Haggadah*)

The first point that the Malbim makes is a very obvious one, why is this passage written in Aramaic and not in Hebrew? He gives an historical answer which is that the ordinary Jew spoke Aramaic and so the invitation to come and eat would be understood by everyone. The Malbim says that to prevent the embarrassment of the poor by an invitation to come and eat, the passage begins with a general historical statement about the origins of eating Matzah and the Mitzvah of doing so. I particularly like the Malbim's view of Ha Lachma Anya being in Aramaic so even children would understand what was going on.

The second commentary is that of the current Chief Rabbi Lord Sacks' Haggadah, my mum's favourite interpretation. Lord Sacks does not discuss the history behind the text but rather the lessons we can learn from it and incorporate into modern life. He says that the Matzah is the food of slaves but also the food that the Israelites ate as a newly freed nation. Lord Sacks continues by telling the story told by Primo Levi of survivors sharing their tiny morsels of bread in Auschwitz. This act of sharing is a message of hope and part of acting as a free person.

---

1    Rabbi Meir Leibush ben Yechiel Michel (1809 - 1879), known by the acronym "Malbim". His Haggadah is published by Targum Press.

I move finally to the choice of my brother and myself, *The Family Participation Haggadah: A Different Night*[2] and its sequel. It refers to a famous medieval commentator, Rabbi Ovadia Seforno[3], who described the Matzah as the original "fast food", as Matzah must be made in under 18 minutes. Another sweet idea is that the text talks about those who are in need as well as those who are hungry, to include at the table not only those who are materially poor but also those who are poor in other ways. For example, as the Haggadah says, this could include those who do not know how to make a Seder or who may be lonely at Pesach. A sequel[4] to The Family Participation Haggadah expands on this point and talks about the unity of the Jews through Ha Lachma Anya.

But how can I, a 15 year old student, relate to this plain yet powerful text? All the materialistic ideas floating around in modern society can make us focus on ourselves and forget that once we were a nation who survived on simple flour and water, that we are all connected with one another. Maybe as a moody, internet addicted teenager I can find a way to revert back to the simple things in life and experience something together with other people. Isn't that what life should be about?

'Bread of our affliction'

2      This Haggadah was edited by Noam Zion and David Dishon and published by the Shalom Hartman Institute.

3      Biblical commentator, 1475-1550.

4      A Night to Remember: The Haggadah of Contemporary Voices by Mishael Zion and Noam Zion. Published by Zion Holiday Publications.

ASKING
QUESTIONS

# Questions Questions
# Ma Nishtana (the Four Questions)

*Helena Sharpstone, Vice Chair of Governors at Wolfson Hillel Primary School and member of Cockfosters and N. Southgate United Synagogue*

So now we come to the part of the Seder which can signal a time for contrasting emotions. After weeks of learning, preparation, and earnest dress rehearsals the youngest child present (usually) takes centre stage to recite the Four Questions in front of extended family and friends. In fact, anybody, not just a child, can lead the reading of the Four Questions and it is good practice for others present to read along in an undertone, either in Hebrew or in English. In my family, some take to this like ducks to water (me), some are shyer but competent and others are so overcome with emotion and nerves that they end up mouthing silently with everyone else singing along. What does it matter? We love them anyway. So take the pressure off the tinies for a minute and consider why we get them to do to the Ma Nishtana in the first place.

The Seder is all about questions and answers. As well as keeping up interest levels, it helps us to remember and retell the story of our journey from slavery to freedom. Even the four questions follow this theme, with the first two relating to slavery and the last two illustrating freedom. Here are a couple of fascinating facts. Did you know the original Ma Nishtana contained only three questions – the fourth one was added later? In addition, one of the questions changed. It used to be about cooking methods. "Why on all other nights may we eat meat which has been roasted, stewed, or boiled, but on this night we eat only roasted meat?" This was a reference to the sacrificing of a lamb on Pesach during the time of the Temple; however, following the destruction of the Temple, the question was changed. So now we ask why we are encouraged to lean on this night. Leaning represents freedom – in those days only a free man had time to recline. If your family is anything like my family, you will be reclining against a variety of bedroom pillows, scatter cushions and rolled up blankets. Not the last word in interior design, but fabulously comfortable and symbolic.

Each person in each generation puts their own unique stamp on the reciting of the Ma Nishtana – that is what makes it such a special part of the Seder. Enjoy.

# Avadim Hayinu –
# We were slaves...

*Paul Martin, a member of Highgate United Synagogue,*
*foreign correspondent and film maker*

We were slaves to Egypt and in many ways we still are. Slaves to the pursuit of goals which may sometimes be dubious, rather than pursuing good deeds and devoting time and energy to family and community. The slavery referred to here took place in "Mitzrayim", the Hebrew name for Egypt. The name "Mitzrayim" is derived from the word "metzer", a limitation; it denotes freedom from limitations.

Of course, we do need to limit some things in life. In fact, Pirkei Avot (ethical teachings in the Mishna, one of the foundation texts of Jewish law and ethics) recommends the need to limit unnecessary activities. By focusing too much on material and external things, the ancient Egyptians were limiting their world view, looking outwards to superficialities rather than to inner truths and values.

We are all limited in certain ways, but there are some limitations that we can not only overcome but can even use to our advantage.

Even being 'in captivity' can even provide opportunities. There are still choices to be made; to stand up to pressure with equanimity, to realise that although you are being put under pressure, you have the choice to maintain your own dignity and integrity, through remaining true to yourself.

I once met a professor who was demoted to a toilet cleaner in Czechoslovakia after Soviet intervention crushed those involved in the relatively liberal revolt called the Prague Spring in 1968. I asked her how she felt as she scrubbed the toilets. "Very good," she said. "Because I realised that although they had brought me to the lowest of the low, I was still me. They couldn't break me." She went on to help lead the 1989 revolt that ended Communist rule in Czechoslovakia. Her words and example were invaluable to me when, on assignment in the Middle East, I found myself in captivity a year ago. I was grateful to feel a similar sense of quiet dignity and triumph over adversity. At one stage, I was placed in a tiny dark cell with a mosquito-infested hole for a toilet, nothing to read or do, and (apart from the three-hour company of a torture victim) was in total isolation.

However, my jailers could not stop me thinking about my priorities in what little might have remained of my life, they could not stop me praying and they could not stop me being me. Overcoming your limitations helps you to focus on what really matters, and to live each second of life to the full. That is freedom, not slavery.

# The Four Children

*Joe Burchell, Chairman of Trustees of Catford & Bromley Synagogue (Affiliated)*

Last Pesach, I had the pleasure of my four grandchildren around the Seder Table. It is inevitable on these family occasions that my mind goes back to when I was in their position. In our case, some of the Haggadot (plural of Haggadah) we have are the same ones that we used all those years ago, wine stained with Matzah pieces still evident in some of the pages, as one of the oldest stories in Jewish History is told. The questions of the 4 children are particularly evocative of Seder nights past.

Here are four questions of my own that I have thought of to help analyse the questions of the four children.

The Wise Child: The answer to his question is, as we know, to teach him the laws of Pesach, particularly, that the Afikoman is the last thing we eat on Seder night. However the wise son's question includes a quote from the Torah, "What are the various laws and judgments that the Lord our God has commanded you?", (Devarim 6:20). Why now, at the Seder specifically, does he ask an apparently general question rather than at any other festival or service?

The Wicked Child: Is this son so wicked by asking, "What do you mean by this service?", (Shemot 12:26)? Is it his rejection, or alternatively, is it his acceptance of the deliverance from Egypt? Why does he ask this specifically at the Seder rather than at any other time?

The Simple Child: Is this son simple or just inquisitive? The verse cited in relation to his question, "What is this?" (Shemot 13:14) surely just demonstrates a thirst for knowledge. Why do we answer him with another verse, "By strength of hand, God brought us out from the house of slavery", (Shemot 13:14)?

The Child who is unable to ask: Is he truly unable to ask? Maybe this means that an opportunity to ask has not yet arrived or that the child has not yet thought to ask. If so, a parent or other adult must take the initiative, hence the verse we quote teaching that, "You shall tell your child on that day, saying, it is because of what God did for me when I came out of Israel" (Shemot 13:8). The Seder night is a time par excellence to take the initiative.

The import of this verse is not solely for a parent and a child; we are all both teachers and students (i.e. parents and children) on Seder night, looking to each other and to our Haggadot for inspiration.

# Rabban Gamliel Haya Omer – Rabban Gamliel Used to Say…

*Rabbi Dr. Michael Harris, The Hampstead Synagogue*

The source of this crucial section of the Haggadah is the Mishna in Arvei Pesachim, the celebrated final chapter of Tractate Pesachim 116a-b, whose subject is the Seder night. Rabban Gamliel, a leader of the rabbinical court in the first and second centuries of the Common Era, identifies three items which are so central that, if they are not explained at the Seder, one has not fulfilled the obligation to tell the story of the Exodus.

An obvious question concerns the order in which Rabban Gamliel places the three items. Chronologically, of course, the Egyptian enslavement of our people preceded the redemption. So why doesn't Maror, representing that enslavement, come first?

One answer, suggested by the Chassidic master Rabbi Simcha Bunim of Pshischah (18th and 19th centuries), is that only after deliverance from suffering can one truly recognise its depth and bitterness. So the Maror has to come last – we can only really taste it having first consumed the Matzah of freedom. This rings true in terms of experience. Often people somehow muster extraordinary strength and fortitude in a crisis; only afterwards do they appreciate the depth of the predicament in which they found themselves - and are then astonished at how they coped.

One might also suggest that the Maror comes last because sadly, its taste lingered through millennia of Jewish history long after the Egyptian experience – through Crusades, Inquisitions, pogroms and the Holocaust. Yet, despite such persecution – and this is a key message of the Seder – God ensures that the Jewish people always survives. The redemption from Egypt is only the first redemption, not the ultimate one.

# 'Mitechila'–FromTheBeginning: surveying the beginnings of the Jewish people

*Daniel Raphael Silverstein, a member of The Hampstead Synagogue*

On Seder night, there is a Mitzvah to retell the story of the Exodus from Egypt. But at what point does that story begin? According to the sage Shmuel (Tractate Pesachim 116a), the story is simple: we were slaves to Pharaoh and then God liberated us – so the beginning is 'Avadim Hayinu' ('we were slaves') which seems to make perfect sense.

Yet for Shmuel's colleague, Rav, this section 'Mitechila' is the real start. We read in this section a quote from Joshua, speaking to the people shortly after they crossed the River Jordan, telling them that our ancestors 'always lived on the other side of the river'. He is reminding them, and us, that that their story, which is also our story, began with Abraham becoming a Hebrew or 'Ivri' – literally 'one who has crossed over'. So what does this tell us about Shmuel's perspective on the story?

Abraham's crossing over 'from the other side' set an example for his descendants to be active in seeking both physical and spiritual freedom. Joshua is reminding the people, and the Haggadah is reminding us, of our responsibility to continue this quest for meaning.

Whereas for Shmuel, the essence of the story is the actual liberation from Egypt, Rav sees the story more strongly in the context of this trans-generational 'crossing over' to seek purpose. Of course, both perspectives have much to teach us, and so the Haggadah weaves both threads of the narrative together, creating a tapestry with many layers of meaning.

FROM
GENERATION TO
GENERATION

# Bechol Dor VaDor - In Every Generation

*Gabriel Herman, Community Development Director at The Hampstead Synagogue*

We are all born into a new generation. I entered the world long after the Holocaust era and twenty odd years after the creation of the modern State of Israel. Each year at Seder, I find it particularly easy to 'feel as if I had actually gone out from Egypt'. I see the Haggadah and the story of Exodus as the loudest of historical echoes.

It does not take a great leap of imagination to see the Nazi terror mirroring that of the ancient Egyptians. But who was the 'Moses' of the Second World War? Is it not incredible that King George VI should have found himself leading the free world against Fascism? A reluctant and unexpected leader who also had to fight a speech impediment? Just like Moses himself.

Likewise, Israel's establishment in 1948 is an echo of the birth of biblical Israel. Many of the defenders of Israel in 1948 were weakened Holocaust survivors whose strength came from remembering how the Angel of Death had passed over their heads. They were determined that it would never happen again.

Somewhere in this interpretation of modern Jewish history, I detect the hand of the Almighty. As all Jews know ... 'in every generation, there are those who rise up to destroy us, but the Holy One, blessed be He, saves us from their hand'. That has always remained true.

SPOTLIGHT ON
THE TEN
PLAGUES

# Plagues in Groups
## Rabbi Michael Laitner

We have just recited the ten plagues and associated Midrashim (early Rabbinic commentaries on the Torah) which explain religious messages of the plagues. Why then does the Haggadah include the Talmudic sage Rabbi Yehudah's grouping of the plagues and why would Rabbi Yehudah do this?

In his commentary, Rashbatz[1] explains that Rabbi Yehudah's intention was to create acronyms for his students so that they would not confuse the order of the plagues.

Why would this be necessary? Rashbatz cites Psalm 78 (in particular verses 44-51) which lists the plagues in a different order to that found in the Torah, perhaps to provide a different perspective on the impact of the plagues, such as, for example, grouping those plagues which were preceded by a warning (see the commentary of Malbim to Psalm 78).

Intriguingly, Nechama Leibowitz[2], one of the foremost Tanach (Bible) educators of the 20th century, cites the great Iberian commentator Rabbi Don Isaac Abravanel[3], who notes Pharaoh's response to Moses in Shemot/Exodus 5:2. In that verse, Pharaoh states three challenges, a) Who is God?, b) Why should I listen to God? c) Why should I obey God? Abravanel says that each group of plagues answered Pharaoh's three statements of defiance. According to this, Rabbi Yehudah's "plagues in groups" teaches an important understanding of the power of God. Plug this into the normal list of plagues and see what you come up with.

---

1      Acronym for Rav Shimon ben Rav Tzemach Duran, 1361-1444.
2      See STUDIES ON THE HAGGADAH: From the Teachings of Nechama Leibowitz, Urim Publications.
3      A leading scholar and statesman, 1437-1508, who left Spain with other Jews in the expulsion of 1492.

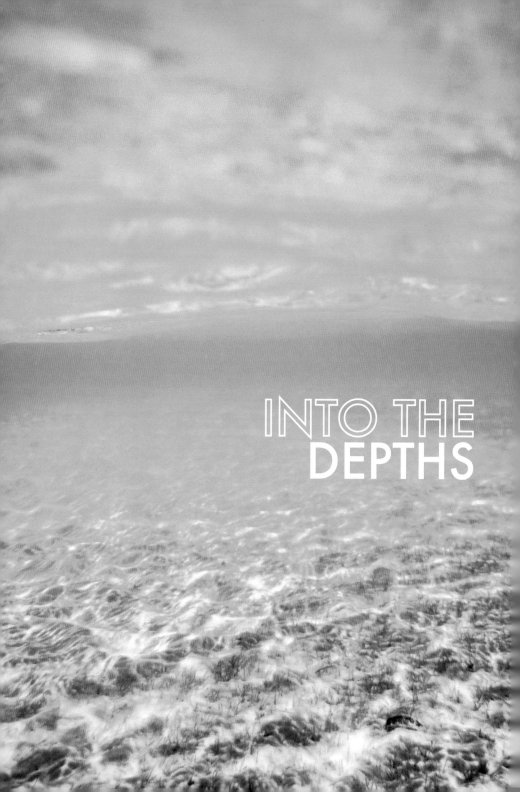

# Yam Suf – the Sea of Reeds

*Simon Goulden, Education Consultant to the United Synagogue and a member of Cockfosters and N. Southgate United Synagogue*

Any study of the geography of the Haggadah would be incomplete without a speculation on the exact location of the events of those momentous times. As we read, the Israelites' first journey is from Ramesses to Sukkot (Shemot/Exodus 12:37). Ramesses is generally identified by archeologists with modern Qantir, the site of Per-Ramesses, the 19th dynasty capital, close to ancient Avaris, about 100km North East of modern Cairo and Sukkot with Tel el-Maskhuta in Wadi Tumilat, in the biblical Land of Goshen, closer to the Suez Canal. From Sukkot the Israelites traveled to Etam "on the edge of the desert," (ibid. 13:20) then turned back to Pi haChirot, directly opposite Ba'al Zephon (ibid 14:2). To date, none of these have been identified with any certainty, but one widely held view is that the Sea of Reeds can be identified with Lake Timsah, a little north of the Gulf of Suez. In ancient times, Lake Timsah was connected to Pithom by a canal, and an old text refers to Migdol Baal Zephon as a fort on the canal, so this looks promising.

In Hebrew, the term for the crossing point is Yam Suph, mistranslated for at least two thousand years from the Greek Septuagint as RED SEA as, in Hebrew, suph never means "red" but rather "reed" or "reeds" (see, for example, the Chief Rabbi's translation in the green Siddur).

# THE END
# GAME

# Enough Is Enough – A closer look at Dayeinu

## Avi Friedmann, Programmes Manager for Tribe and US Living & Learning

One of the most recognisable tunes of the Seder is Dayeinu, the song about God delivering the Jewish people from slavery in Egypt. Despite being one of the first songs we learn as children in preparation for the Seder, its meaning is so multi-faceted that it succinctly tells the Exodus story in full.

Nobody knows exactly where or when Dayeinu originated and was incorporated into the Haggadah, although it has been around since at least the ninth century CE. The oldest known record of the song in its current format is found in the Seder Rav Amram[1], a siddur and volume of poetry which was the magnum opus of Rav Amram Gaon (d. 857CE). However, it is notable that by the late twelfth century, it had not yet found its way into the liturgy of Maimonides's *Nusach Hahaggadah* (text of the Haggadah)[2].

Each of Dayeinu's fifteen stanzas recounts a momentous act of benevolence that God bestowed on us as He led His nation on history's most celebrated journey. The song can be divided into three clear groups: the first five stanzas describe the Exodus, followed by the middle five which describe miraculous aspects of the journey itself and dwelling in the wilderness. The final five end the song by listing five ways that God brought the Jewish people close to Him.

However the one odd feature of Dayeinu is the nature of its message. Dayeinu literally means "that would have been enough for us." The suggestion is that if God had performed only the first, or each of these successive miracles for the Jewish people, this would have been enough.

The pattern of "that would have been enough for us" continues throughout the song, so that, peculiarly, each line specifically states that were God not to have performed each successive miracle, it would have sufficed. Are we suggesting that God did too much? Are we audacious enough to suggest that we would have preferred only to have been freed and neither to have received the Torah nor to have come close enough to God, and worship Him according to His commandments? These are difficult questions that challenge our very approach to the message of the Seder and even our with God.

---

1    Folktales of the Jews: Tales from Eastern Europe: Vol. II (Jewish Publication Society of America, 2007), p.383.
2    Rambam La'am (Ktav Yad): Vol. Zmanim B, Nusach HaHagadah, (Mossad Harav Kook, 1946) p. 444-450. Maimonides (Rabbi Moshe ben Maimon), 1135-1204, is also known by the acronym "Rambam".

To answer these testing questions, it is important to recognise that the Jewish attitude to such challenges is positive and engaging. A fundamental principle of Rabbinic discourse is that of "machloket leshaim shamayim", (dispute in the name of heaven); meaning that Judaism finds its routes in such challenges. We grapple with questions about our faith and our relationship with God in order to strengthen our faith and that relationship. This operates with the all important caveat of "leshaim shamayim" (for the sake of Heaven) always ensuring the purpose of such explorations is to become closer to God and to understand how to keep His mitzvot better.

In search of a solution to our question, we shall recall a curious rabbinic debate recorded in the Talmud[3]. For two and a half years, the leading academies of their time, "Beit Hillel" and "Beit Shammai", debated whether mankind would have been better off having never been created. Beit Shammai argued for the motion, whilst Beit Hillel argued against. In the end the Sanhedrin (Rabbinic High Court) voted, perhaps surprisingly, in favor of Beit Shammai ruling that mankind would have been better off had it not been created in the first place (for that way we would never have sinned); since though we actually have been created, we should "examine our actions", with the clear implication that we should improve our actions.

That such a dispute is recorded in the Talmud immediately absolves our concerns about the legitimacy of our question about Dayeinu. It also serves as an answer.

The root of this Talmudic debate is the very essence of a Jew's search for meaning. Do I truly have free will in the face of my covenant with God to keep His laws? How do I reconcile my humility in God's presence with my hopes and dreams? The Yom Kippur liturgy[4] emphasises that before the Creator we are nothing. Yet we also learn of God's benevolence and desire for us to achieve "devekut" (closeness to Him[5]). As we shall see, these two seemingly contradictory ideas can be reconciled.

This helps to understand the tension that exists beneath the familiar words and tune of Dayeinu. This poetic account of the Jewish journey to find God in the

---

3       Babylonian Talmud, Tractate Eruvin, 13b.

4       "True! For You are their creator, and You know their desires, for they are (but) flesh and blood. Man: his roots are from dust and his end is to dust. For his very soul he makes his bread. He is likened to a smashed sword, a dry field, a dying flower bud, a passing shade, a disintegrating cloud, a howling wind, a dust storm, and a fleeting dream." Machzor Rabbah: Yom Kippur, p.326 (translation is my own).

5       Whilst devekut is usually expressed as the Hasidic expression of the desire to be close to God with its roots in Kaballah, there are also a number of examples throughout the Tanach (Bible) where God expresses the desire for the Jewish people to 'cling' to Him; although for our purposes one example will suffice to make the point: "For just as a loincloth clings to its wearer's loins, so too have I caused all the House of Israel cling to me..." Jeremiah 13:11 (It is noteworthy that this example uses a romanticised literary reference to a loincloth, amplifying the running theme of the Jewish people's relationship with God as that of two lovers, found throughout the books of Neviim (Prophets) and Ketubim (Writings). This also serves as the central theme of the entire book of Song of Songs, which some households have the custom to read at the end of the Seder.)

wilderness, and our commitment to keep His commandments is born of a deep humility. The inner struggle to find purpose is answered by God in His longing for His people to be close to him through the Torah. We recognise that we were not worthy of freedom from Egypt, let alone receiving the Torah or the building of the holy Temple in Jerusalem. This song is not an audacious wish for freedom from "Ol Malchut Shamayim" (the yolk of the royal majesty of Heaven). Instead, it is a celebration of majesty. The Torah is a gift from God, serving to enable us to celebrate a close bond with God and to honour our covenant with Him.

*'God led His nation from slavery to freedom...'*

God led His nation from slavery to freedom with "an outstretched arm"[6] to bring us closer to Him. Adherence to God's laws is the ultimate expression of our loyalty and gratitude, but it is also the method through which we cling to Him, reassured by the reciprocal nature of our covenant with Him. That reciprocal nature provides that God's providence throughout the journey of the Jewish people across the ages is the affirmation of a close, mutual, bond. We have an eternal covenant with God.

This helps us to understand how we can say "Dayeinu". We would have thanked God for each stage of Dayeinu by itself, knowing that God's covenant with us is unbreakable. We also thank God for His benevolence to us, knowing that even when we are unworthy, God is with us, as hard as this may feel sometimes. This combination helps us to continue through the fifteen lines of Dayeinu and to complete the song.

---

6     Shemot/Exodus 6:6.

THEREFORE
WE ARE OBLIGED
TO THANK

# Lefichach – לפיכך - Therefore...
## Rabbi Harvey Belovski, Golders Green United Synagogue

Therefore, we are obliged to thank…

This section appears soon before the meal when thoughts may be on other things! Its basic meaning is straightforward: we must praise God for all of the miracles of the Exodus; it introduces Hallel, which follows directly afterwards. However, the first word, "lefichach" (therefore), is intriguing – therefore what?

The key to understanding this is establishing that the Haggadah is not a jumble of loosely-connected texts about the Exodus, but a carefully-crafted sequence of inspirational ideas that reaches its culmination as the story-telling draws to a close. The previous passage tells us that in every generation, each of us must imagine ourselves actually leaving Egypt during the Seder. That is the real goal of the first half of the evening – to tell the story in a manner so vivid and transformational for the participants, that they feel themselves transported to a world in which they are lifelong slaves about to experience the first precious taste of freedom.

In fact, in many Sephardi homes, the participants actually act out parts of the story for this reason. So we are back in Egypt, with the pyramids on the horizon, the Egyptian taskmasters just a memory, and our paragraph demands: 'therefore'! Note the phrase 'for our ancestors and for us', connecting it with the theme of the previous section. The Haggadah commentary attributed to Rashi's[1] grandson, Rabbi Shmuel, says succinctly: since it is as though we ourselves have come out from Egypt, we are obliged to sing praises, just as our ancestors did.

[1] Rabbi Shlomo ben Yitzchak (acronym: Rashi). C.1040-1105, wrote the foremost commentaries to the Torah (Pentateuch) and Talmud (main body of Jewish law).

# STEPPING
# THROUGH
# THE LOOKING
# GLASS

# First part of Hallel in the Haggadah

*Doreen Samuels, member of Pinner United Synagogue, a Bradfield Graduate and a leading Jewish education consultant*

Many people try to find an original addition to the traditional Four Questions each year. Here's one: Which part of the Shacharit (morning) prayer service is included in our Seder service?

The answer is Hallel, which is recited on Yom Tov (festivals), with the exception of Rosh Hashana and Yom Kippur. Hallel is also recited on Rosh Chodesh (the marking of a new month).

We have almost finished the "Maggid" section of the Haggadah, telling and retelling the age-old story; we are about to drink the second cup of wine, and then immediately following the "Lefichach" paragraph, without any warning or explanation, we sing the first two Tehilim (Psalms) of Hallel, finishing the rest of Hallel after our meal. Why?

The answer lies embedded in the paragraphs of "B'chol dor va'dor" and "Lefichach" which precede Hallel: God did not only save our ancestors from Egypt, He saved us with them.

At this point, the Seder shifts into a different gear. We are no longer telling a story – we are experiencing our own redemption. We have stepped through the Looking Glass – no longer spectators but participants in the miracle.

The first two Tehillim of Hallel are Psalms 113 and 114; their words are so compelling on this night of freedom from Egyptian slavery.

Psalm 113 begins by addressing us as "Avdei Hashem", servants of God, no longer "Avadim", physical slaves,  as we are described in the Haggadah's first response to "Ma Nishtana" – nor spiritual slaves, nor 'Avdei Avodah Zarah', idol worshippers, as described by the great Talmudic sage, Rav.

Psalm 114 describes our spiritual journey from Egypt to our acceptance of God's sovereignty.

With hearts full of joy, we praise and thank God at the tops of our voices for saving us, for giving us a place at this table, at this time, for enabling us to experience anew that maelstrom of emotions that tells us we are free people, a people free to serve God.

TASTING
BITTERNESS

# Maror (bitter herbs)

## Ayala Hirst, a member of Alei Tzion United Synagogue

The famous Talmudic sage Rabban Gamliel says one must discuss Maror in order to fulfil the obligation of Pesach study, as we read in our Haggadot. "These bitter herbs that we eat, what are they for?", he asks. Like the preceding paragraphs describing the Pesach offering (Pascal lamb) and the eating of Matzah, the Maror paragraph presumes that we are already in the midst of the action, in this case, eating Maror. The phrasing of this question is significant since the eating itself is not being questioned. We hope to learn the rationale for eating Maror, but our observance is not dependant on our understanding.

We eat bitter herbs to taste the bitterness that we felt as Egyptian slaves. Nechama Leibowitz[1] teaches that a seemingly superfluous final phrase of the pasuk (verse) in Shemot/Exodus 1:14 quoted here in the Haggadah points to the extent of our bitterness. In addition to being slaves to Pharaoh, we also did the mundane work for all of the Egyptians. Even the Egyptian maids who were at sharpest end of society, enslaved us according to Rashi[2] (Shemot 11:5). All strands of Egyptian society had a hand in our oppression.

The choice of bitter herb speaks of our experience in Egypt. Romaine lettuce, which is also suitable to be eaten for Maror, initially tastes sweet but leaves a bitter aftertaste. The lettuce will be more bitter the longer it grows in the ground. This is analogous to our experience in Egypt. When Jacob's family first came to Egypt, their lives were rich. Joseph was viceroy and they were given one of the best areas in Egypt, Goshen. But while they may have started as elite members of society they ultimately became poor oppressed slaves living embittered lives.

However, based on this experience, the Sefat Emet[3] in his article on Pesach, (1873) suggests the profound idea that bitterness serves as fuel for freedom. When we felt pain in Egypt it was a subtle first call for change to become free people and to connect more with God. Tasting the bitterness at the Seder table reminds us of the pain we felt, how we ached for God to redeem us and build us into a nation as ultimately happened after the Exodus.

---

1      Nechama Leibowitz (1905-1997) was born in Riga and moved to Israel in 1930. Her teaching style and weekly Bible study sheets made her one of the most significant Judaic teachers of the twentieth century. She has thousands of students all over the world.

2      Acronym for Rabbi Shlomo ben Yitzchak (1040-1105), the foremost Biblical commentator.

3      Rabbi Yehuda Leib Alter, (1847-1905) second Rebbe of the "Gerer" Chasidic group. Rabbi Alter is often referred to as the "Sefat Emet", the name of his most popular work.

HILLEL
SANDWICH
KORECH

# Korech

*Rica Infante, Vice Chair, Sutton & District United Synagogue*

The renowned Talmudic sage Hillel instituted Korech, a sandwich of Matzah and Maror (bitter herbs) during the Second Temple period, as a symbolic reminder of the hasty exodus from Egypt, coupled with the bitterness of slavery that our forefathers endured there.

Rabbi Gideon Weitzman explores the concepts that Hillel applied when eating Korech. He states:

"Hillel comes to teach us that in order to truly understand the suffering we need to fuse it together with the freedom;"[1] in other words, in order to appreciate one you must have experienced the other.

Hillel's rationale in the context of our world today is that freedom cannot ever be taken for granted because it can be lost in the flicker of an eyelid.

Unfortunately, those who have not experienced political unrest or threatening times may tend to take their freedom as a given. The generations who survived the Holocaust and two World Wars fought against the odds so their children would enjoy the freedom they and their generation lost.

It is up to each and every Jew who eats Korech at the Seder to thank God and our forefathers for the miracle that is Israel, both the people and the land, and to think what we can all do for them both.

---

1      Light of Redemption : A Passover Haggadah based on the Writings of Rav Kook (66:2:3-4) Rabbi Gideon Weitzman; Grow Publications, Jerusalem www.GrowingJewish.com

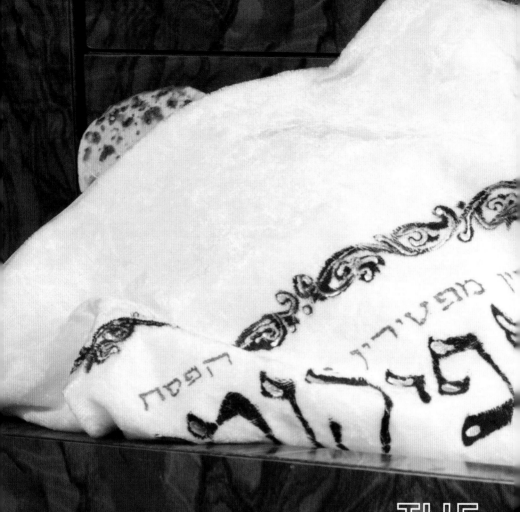

# THE
# AFIKOMAN

# The Afikoman

*Rabbi Yitzchok Schochet, Mill Hill United Synagogue*

The common custom of hiding the Afikoman is, in keeping with other rituals at the Seder, primarily to encourage children to remain awake. A central mitzvah of the Seder night is, "and you shall tell it to your children,"[1] hence we endeavour to pique their curiosity throughout. There is a wider message contained therein, for just as the child goes in search of this humble bread and is rewarded upon finding it, so we must have sufficient humility constantly to search and explore the depths of our faith, whereby we will be rewarded by discovering the deeper truths within.

The Afikoman is created from the middle Matzah broken into halves at the onset of the Seder. This middle Matzah corresponds to the middle Patriarch, Isaac, who, according to Kabbalah, represents the attribute of Divine judgement. The breaking of the Matzah signifies the 'sweetening' of this judgement. This 'sweetening' then manifests itself in the Afikoman which is a combination of the words "afiku man – bringing out mannah", that is, an emanation of nourishment signifying the attribute of Divine compassion. Thus the Afikoman marks the culmination of recounting the Exodus at the Seder, as we look to make the transition from the judgement of our current state of exile to the compassionate fulfilment of the Divine promise, "as in the days I took you out from Egypt, I will once again show you wonders."[2]

---

1       Shemot/Exodus 13:8.
2       Micha 7:15.

# *Final words*

*Rabbi Andrew Shaw, Director of US Living & Learning and Community Development Rabbi at Stanmore & Canons Park Synagogue*

Remembering my childhood, it was always the most magical night of the year. The guests arrived and I was allowed to stay up way past my bed time. I will never forget the first time I sang Ma Nishtana, or the time I got my first hamster as a prize for finding the Afikoman!

Seder night is the most superb educational experience appealing to all of our five senses. We see the wide variety of colourful Haggadot at the table, we smell the various foods of the night, we taste the bitterness of the Maror and the saltiness of the egg. We hear the ancient and still yet modern words and tunes of Seder night.

But what about touch? Yes, I suppose we touch the Matzah and the Haggadot but for me the sense of touch on Seder night is actually reversed. We do not touch Seder night, instead Seder night touches every one of our hearts and our souls. It is the story of a people who were lifted from slavery to freedom, and not just any people – our people. It is not just any story – it is our story.

To be a part of an event, a ceremony that goes back millennia is for me inspiring in an age where things are changing rapidly. To hold the wine and declare 'bechol dor va dor amad aleinu l'chalotenu,' ('in every generation they arose to destroy us'), to realise that despite that being unfortunately true, we have managed not only to survive but also to return to our homeland and build the third Jewish commonwealth. Le shanah ha ba'ah birushalayim – may we be next year in Jerusalem, in fulfilment of the Bible's words.

However, Seder night also brings with it the message of the "fifth child" in addition to the better known four children of the Seder. This fifth child is the child, or any other person, who is not at the Seder table, the person that has drifted away. How can this person come home, back to the Seder table? The answer is to be found on the Seder night itself, close to home. Throughout the year, we need to make Jewish education transformative, experiential and alive – just like it is on Seder night. We cannot simply learn our Judaism; we need to live it with passion, with drive and with vigour. This may yet bring the fifth child back whilst enhancing our own lives at the same time. We must be living and learning our Judaism. We hope that this Guide has helped to advance that process for Pesach and onwards.

The Living & Learning Department at the US looks forward to working together with your community in the coming months in this vein.

Chag Sameach from us all.

Rabbi Andrew Shaw